# Unleashing Productivity through Firm Financing

Tatiana Didier and Ana Paula Cusolito

# Contents

## Tables

# Foreword

Small and medium enterprises (SMEs) employ a large share of the global workforce and are among the most important contributors to job creation and economic development around the world. However, SMEs face a range of obstacles that hinder their capacity to invest and innovate, which in turn, hampers their critical role as engines of economic growth. Access to finance is a primary constraint for SME growth, particularly in emerging market and developing economies (EMDEs). SMEs tend to resort to internal funding rather than external financing. For example, estimates in this volume show that the small firms have debt-to-asset (leverage) ratios of around 65 percent in high-income countries (HICs), whereas similarly sized firms in middle-income countries (MICs) have leverage ratios of about 40 percent. Moreover, those SMEs that can borrow often face exorbitantly high interest rates, despite being some of the most productive firms in their respective markets.

While the COVID-19 pandemic has brought renewed attention to the enabling role of financing for firms, there is remarkably little discussion about how financial constraints affect firm dynamics, and little understanding of the impact on jobs, economic growth, productivity, and overall prosperity. This is a fundamental concern for policy makers and an imperative for the design of effective support policies. For example, policy makers must consider how firms secure funding throughout their life cycles. Which firms are facing critical financing shortfalls? What are the underlying causes for these gaps? How do financial constraints impact resource allocation among firms, and how do they influence the expansion, improvement, and resilience of existing firms? Crafting effective policies in the face of glaring financing disparities for firms is an essential challenge that policy makers must confront.

This comprehensive volume, *Unleashing Productivity through Firm Financing*, provides new evidence on the channels through which financial constraints for firms, particularly SMEs, impinge on countries' economic growth and productivity. There is a direct relation between firm financing and firm performance. Restricted access to finance has a negative impact on firm growth, investments, and job creation. While access to equity financing can be invaluable in fostering innovation-driven growth, many EMDEs often have underdeveloped equity markets, with debt being the primary source of financing for firms. Furthermore, a new data set comprising 2.5 million firms across MICs and HICs shows misallocation of finance as costly for MICs. In fact, MICs could obtain gains in aggregate productivity, which would measure firms' ability to produce more with less, of up to 86 percent by reducing firms' financing gaps, particularly for SMEs. MICs with lower gross domestic product per capita would see the largest gains. In addition, access to diversified sources of financing helps firms better manage risks, allowing them to reduce job losses and maintain investment levels. For instance, firms in EMDEs that had access to financing during the COVID-19 pandemic preserved more jobs.

The research presented here is part of the World Bank's Productivity Project. We hope policy makers, researchers, and development practitioners will find value in the fresh insights presented here. We encourage them to further explore the wide range of issues raised and bridge the critical knowledge gaps.

Jean Pesme
Global Director, Finance
Finance, Competitiveness, and
Innovation Global Practice
World Bank

# Preface from the Series Editor

Productivity accounts for half of the differences in gross domestic product per capita across countries. Identifying policies that stimulate productivity is thus critical to alleviating poverty and fulfilling the rising aspirations of global citizens. In recent decades, however, productivity growth has slowed globally, and the lagging productivity performance of developing countries is a major barrier to convergence with income levels in high-income countries. The World Bank Productivity Project seeks to bring frontier thinking to the measurement and determinants of productivity, grounded in the developing country context, to global policy makers. Each volume in the series explores a different aspect of the topic, fostering a dialogue among academics and policy makers through sponsored empirical work in the World Bank's client countries.

*Unleashing Productivity through Firm Financing*, the eighth and final volume in the series, does not aspire to offer a distillation of the frontier literature on the links between finance and productivity growth. It rather offers empirical confirmation, in many cases for the first time, that this literature corresponds tightly to the realities of the developing world as well. The major advance is the construction of a data set of 2.5 million private firms across middle- and high-income countries. This permits exploration that was heretofore not possible of the channels through which financial frictions, distortions, and market failures constrain firm performance and the efficient allocation of resources across firms. Further, this volume documents that these effects are large—mitigating them potentially can double aggregate productivity in middle-income countries—and particularly detrimental to small firms. This volume also characterizes the importance of debt versus equity for different types of firm activities.

The combined findings of this volume and those of the previous volumes in the series show that the innovation, growth, agricultural productivity, entrepreneurship, service sector, and technological transfer agendas all depend on deepening and diversifying the financial sector and suggest that the policy interventions discussed here merit being ranked high on the reform agenda.

William F. Maloney
Chief Economist, Latin America and the Caribbean Region
Director, World Bank Productivity Project Series
World Bank

## Other Titles in the World Bank Productivity Project

*Bridging the Technological Divide: Technology Adoption by Firms in Developing Countries.* 2022. Xavier Cirera, Diego Comin, and Marcio Cruz. Washington, DC: World Bank.

*Place, Productivity, and Prosperity: Revisiting Spatially Targeted Policies for Regional Development.* 2022. Arti Grover, Somik V. Lall, and William F. Maloney. Washington, DC: World Bank.

*At Your Service? The Promise of Services-Led Development.* 2021. Gaurav Nayyar, Mary Hallward-Driemeier, and Elwyn Davies. Washington, DC: World Bank.

*Harvesting Prosperity: Technology and Productivity Growth in Agriculture.* 2020. Keith Fuglie, Madhur Gautam, Aparajita Goyal, and William F. Maloney. Washington, DC: World Bank.

*High-Growth Firms: Facts, Fiction, and Policy Options for Emerging Economies.* 2019. Arti Grover Goswami, Denis Medvedev, and Ellen Olafsen. Washington, DC: World Bank.

*Productivity Revisited: Shifting Paradigms in Analysis and Policy.* 2018. Ana Paula Cusolito and William F. Maloney. Washington, DC: World Bank.

*The Innovation Paradox: Developing-Country Capabilities and the Unrealized Promise of Technological Catch-Up.* 2017. Xavier Cirera and William F. Maloney. Washington, DC: World Bank.

All books in the World Bank Productivity Project are available free of charge at https://openknowledge.worldbank.org/handle/10986/30560.

# Acknowledgments

This book was written by Tatiana Didier (senior economist, World Bank) and Ana Paula Cusolito (senior economist, World Bank). The book builds on analytical work by the authors and a series of background papers that were written specifically for this project. For their contributions, we thank Andrea Castagnola, Brian Castro Aguirre, Beulah Chelva, Subika Farazi, Roberto N. Fattal, Jose Ernesto López Córdova, Davide S. Mare, Sergio Muro, Jorge Pena, and Akshat V. Singh.

The work was carried out under the guidance of Pablo Saavedra (vice president, Prosperity, World Bank), Jean Pesme (global director, Finance, Competitiveness, and Innovation Global Practice, World Bank), and William F. Maloney (director, World Bank Productivity Project, and chief economist, Latin America and the Caribbean Region, World Bank). We also thank Alfonso Garcia Mora (regional vice president, Latin America and the Caribbean and Europe, International Finance Corporation) and Ayhan Kose (chief economist and director, Development Economics and Chief Economist, Prospects Group, World Bank) for their guidance and support at earlier stages of this project in the roles of global director and chief economist, respectively.

We are very thankful to the World Bank peer reviewers who provided key inputs during the concept note review, quality enhancement review, and decision meeting: Randa Akeel (senior financial sector specialist), Steen Byskov (senior financial officer), Ana Fiorella Carvajal (lead financial sector specialist), Robert Cull (research manager), Shanthi Divakaran (senior financial sector specialist), Leonardo Iacovone (lead economist), Mariana Iootty de Paiva Dias (senior economist), Martha Licetti (practice manager), William Maloney (chief economist, Latin America and the Caribbean Region), Andres Martinez (senior financial sector specialist), Martin Melecky (lead economist), Alen Mulabdic (economist), Gaurav Nayyar (lead economist), Ha Nguyen (senior economist), Francesca de Nicola (senior economist), Fausto Patino (economist), Regina Pleninger (economist), Matthew Saal (principal industry specialist), Sergio Schmukler (research manager), Asli Senkal (special assistant), Ilias Skamnelos (practice manager), and Shu Yu (senior economist). We also thank the participants at the authors' workshop, which took place during October–November 2021, who provided useful comments on draft versions of this work.

We thank our publishing team—Patricia Katayama and Mark McClure—for the design, production, and marketing of this book; Nancy Morrison and Sandra Gain for their excellent and timely editorial services; Ann O'Malley for proofreading; and our communications team for its creative energy in promoting the book.

# About the Authors

**Ana Paula Cusolito** is a senior economist in the Finance, Competitiveness, and Innovation Global Practice of the World Bank. Her research focuses on industrial organization, including firm and aggregate productivity as well as its determinants, digital technology adoption, innovation, corporate governance, and foreign competition. She has coauthored World Bank flagship publications, including *World Development Report 2019: The Changing Nature of Work, Productivity Revisited: Shifting Paradigms in Analysis and Policy,* and *The Upside of Digital for the Middle East and North Africa: How Digital Technology Adoption Can Accelerate Growth and Jobs,* among others. Her research has been published in the *American Economic Review: Insights, The Review of Economics and Statistics, Journal of International Economics,* and *Journal of Development Economics,* among others. Before joining the World Bank, she worked at the Inter-American Development Bank as country economist for Costa Rica. She holds a PhD in economics from Universitat Pompeu Fabra, a master's degree from Universidad del Centro de Estudios Macroeconómicos de Argentina, and a bachelor's degree from Universidad Nacional de La Plata.

**Tatiana Didier** is a senior economist in the Finance, Competitiveness, and Innovation Global Practice of the World Bank. Her work focuses on corporate finance and financial sector development, with an emphasis on the challenges for firms in developing countries. She has played a leading role in a number of World Bank country and regional policy engagements. She is also the leading author of several World Bank reports, including *Emerging Issues in Financial Development: Lessons from Latin America* and the forthcoming "Boosting SME Finance for Growth: The Case for More Effective Support Policies." Her research has been published in the *Journal of Monetary Economics, The Review of Economics and Statistics, Journal of International Economics,* and *Journal of Financial Stability,* among others. She has received two World Bank Financial and Private Sector Development Academy Awards for her research. She holds a PhD in economics from the Massachusetts Institute of Technology.

# Executive Summary

This volume provides original empirical evidence that quantifies the so-called small and medium enterprise (SME) financing gap and its sizable negative impact on aggregate outcomes, such as productivity and growth. This has been an elusive feature in discussions of firms' access to finance, especially in emerging market and developing economies (EMDEs). SMEs are considered the backbone of the economy in most EMDEs, but they face critical challenges in access to finance that hinder their potential to create more and better jobs. Drawing from a newly constructed data set of 2.5 million firms across middle-income countries (MICs) and high-income countries (HICs), the volume shows that financial market inefficiencies—namely, financial frictions and market failures—constrain financing to these firms. In turn, this misallocation of finance hinders firms' ability to invest and even use inputs efficiently, thus negatively impacting their performance, and ultimately aggregate productivity and growth. Novel estimates show that mitigating these inefficiencies, thereby relaxing the constraints on firms' access to debt and equity financing, can lead to aggregate productivity gains of up to 86 percent in MICs, with the largest gains observed among MICs with lower gross domestic product (GDP) per capita. These gains stem from a reallocation of financial resources toward financially constrained yet productive firms.

Costly misallocation of finance is particularly detrimental to SMEs, particularly those with fewer than 100 employees that tend to face the largest financing gaps. The estimation results show that smaller firms in MICs would benefit the most from a more efficient allocation of capital across firms. These firms typically face a substantial financing gap in both debt and equity. On average, the smallest private firms in the sample have debt-to-assets (leverage) ratios of around 65 percent in HICs, whereas similarly sized firms in MICs have leverage ratios averaging 40 percent. The smallest private firms in MICs have even lower leverage ratios, around 20 percent, indicating a much more limited use of debt financing. The differential in leverage ratios between firms in MICs and HICs declines with firm size, with virtually no differences observed among the largest private firms and publicly listed firms.

Smaller, innovative private firms in MICs make limited use of both debt and external equity financing. Private markets for equity financing in EMDEs more broadly are significantly underdeveloped, and they tend to be concentrated in financing relatively large firms, which constrains the availability of equity financing for smaller, innovative firms. For example, private firms with more than 350 employees accounted for roughly

70 percent of venture capital investments in MICs during 2010–19, compared to 35 percent in HICs.

Debt is a crucial source of financing for SMEs, but equity financing can be powerful in promoting innovation. Although the estimations show that the misallocation of finance across firms stems in large part from a scale effect (an inefficient allocation of the total amount of finance to firms), the results also indicate that countries with more knowledge- and technology-related outputs, hence an arguably larger share of firms engaging in innovative activities, would benefit the most from improvement in the composition of financing (the allocation of capital between debt and equity). That is, countries with more innovative activities could obtain sizable productivity gains from rebalancing the composition of financing to firms toward greater access to equity finance. These results highlight that firms' capital structure matters for aggregate productivity, at least in part because of the value of equity financing for innovative firms. Yet, venture capital financing is skewed toward a narrow set of high-tech sectors, suggesting that equity financing might play a limited role in advancing technological change in EMDEs.

Financial constraints not only hinder firms' performance but also constrain their ability to cope with adverse shocks. The results in this volume show that during the COVID-19 pandemic, many firms in EMDEs were unable to mitigate the effects of the shock, partly because their access to financing was limited. Firms that had access to financing were better able to maintain employment levels and avoid falling into arrears. Moreover, access to diversified sources of financing can help firms to weather shocks. For example, the results show that capital market financing can replace bank lending during banking crises, allowing firms to mitigate the adverse effects of the crisis on performance and employment. Hence, firms with limited access to multiple sources of financing (whether debt or equity) are more exposed to the effects of negative shocks. For smaller firms in EMDEs, which are often dependent on banks for finance, small fluctuations in bank credit can have sizable effects on their investments and growth.

The original findings in this volume provide strong analytical underpinnings for existing, practical knowledge in supporting SME financing. This volume also has important implications for financial sector policies that address financing gaps for firms in EMDEs. Debt constitutes the largest and most important source of finance for a vast majority of private firms around the world. Hence, the core focus of policy initiatives aimed at fostering firm financing should be on supporting widespread and efficient access to debt financing for SMEs. That is, the targeting of policy support should reflect the more acute financing gaps for smaller firms in a country. Targeted interventions should intentionally focus on addressing key financial market failures and frictions underlying the challenges in access to finance to SMEs, such as improving information on SMEs, "de-risking" SMEs, and developing missing markets.

The direct engagement of private capital in a sustainable manner is critical for the development of firm financing in EMDEs. Policy makers should thus place significant emphasis on improving additionality and crowding in private capital, while minimizing distortions and outright avoiding crowding out effects, when designing targeted support policies. In this regard, clear graduation criteria are essential for the sustainability and effectiveness of targeted policies, ensuring that market-based financing for SMEs develops. Importantly, this size-based targeting in policies should not translate into unconditional support to firms simply based on their size. The viability of firms is critical, for instance, to avoid supporting the proliferation of zombie firms.

Policy support needs to take a differentiated approach for debt and equity financing. Targeting is more complex yet imperative for equity financing, due in large part to the scarcity of this financing source in EMDEs. The targeting of programs for equity financing should go beyond a size-based approach, recognizing that for a subset of SMEs—notably, innovative ones—balanced access to debt and equity financing would be invaluable. The results also suggest that policy interventions to support equity market development are more likely to succeed when certain preconditions are in place, such as the existence of a strong institutional investor base and a supportive entrepreneurial environment. These conditions are more likely to be observed among the more financially developed MICs, raising questions about the effectiveness of interventions in EMDEs more broadly. Overall, policy makers must be cognizant of the trade-offs in allocating resources to support equity financing versus debt financing, while being realistic about the feasibility and impact of policy interventions. This is especially so when fiscal resources are scarce.

A supportive enabling environment is the backbone of firm financing. While not directly targeted on smaller private firms, policies fostering the enabling environment for debt and equity financing tend to entail disproportionate benefits for this set of firms, thereby complementing more targeted interventions. This is the case for policies aimed at strengthening the financial infrastructure, such as credit information systems and insolvency frameworks. On the latter, the estimations show that deficiencies in insolvency systems can distort incentives—for example, by supporting inefficient loan evergreening—that increase the likelihood and prolong the survival of zombie firms. The findings show that weak insolvency systems lock up both capital and labor in low productivity uses. To the extent that labor released from exiting firms is absorbed by more productive firms, there could be significant gains in aggregate output.

In supporting access to finance for firms, policy makers need to consider the unique circumstances of each country and prioritize evidence-based policies that address the challenges of the SME financing gap. A rigorous, data-driven assessment of the key constraints on firm financing and their underlying causes within the context of individual countries is important for the design of policies (for example, to enhance the effectiveness of targeted support policies), as well as for policy implementation (for example, by enabling the implementation of effective monitoring and evaluation frameworks). However, there is a generalized lack of data on the financing of private firms across the developing world, which is particularly marked in countries where data are most needed, such as those with underdeveloped financial systems, where financial inefficiencies can be more constraining. Improving the availability of and access to data is thus crucial for a more effective policy agenda supporting firm financing in EMDEs.

# Abbreviations

| | |
|---|---|
| BPS | Business Pulse Survey |
| EMDEs | emerging market and developing economies |
| FCF | financially constrained firm |
| GDP | gross domestic product |
| GEI | Global Entrepreneurship Index |
| HICs | high-income countries |
| ICT | information and communications technology |
| IPO | initial public offering |
| MENA | Middle East and North Africa |
| MICs | middle-income countries |
| MRPF | marginal revenue product of each factor |
| MSMEs | micro, small, and medium enterprises |
| PE | private equity |
| R&D | research and development |
| SMEs | small and medium enterprises |
| TFP | total factor productivity |
| TFPR | revenue total factor productivity |
| VC | venture capital |

# 1. Analytical Framework

**Key Messages**

- **Differences in aggregate productivity and growth across countries, and hence welfare, can be traced to the performance of the firm—as the engine of the economy.** In turn, firm performance depends on financing. The ability of firms to finance investments in physical capital, managerial capabilities, technological adoption, and innovation generally is central to aggregate outcomes, such as productivity and growth.
- **Access to finance supports firms' performance, and consequently, aggregate productivity and growth, along three margins:** improved performance within the firm (the *within* margin), improved allocation of resources across firms (the *between* margin), and improved dynamics of the entry and exit of firms (the *selection* margin).
- **A myriad of financial market frictions and distortions can prevent an efficient allocation of resources to firms.** Financial constraints can thus hinder firms' ability to use inputs efficiently and constrain firms' investments, productivity, and growth, with potentially sizable impairments to aggregate outcomes. The impact of these frictions and distortions can vary across firms with different attributes, such as firm size and age. They can also affect firms differently depending on the type of activity firms undertake.
- **Corporate financing decisions are often driven by access to finance, both the level and composition of available finance.** Financial frictions and distortions can be mitigated by the type of finance, and thus the choice of contract between firms and investors (notably, equity versus debt). The type of financing can matter a great deal. For instance, the financing of innovative activities critically depends on access to equity financing.
- **This volume focuses on the linkages between firm financing, financial constraints, firm performance, and aggregate outcomes such as productivity and growth.** Using comprehensive data for private firms in high- and middle-income countries, the volume provides for the first time a quantitative assessment of the extent of financial constraints on private firms of different sizes, the role of capital structure, and the impact of such constraints on aggregate growth and productivity.

## Introduction

Firms' ability to finance investments in physical and human capital and innovate through digital, green, and other technologies is central to productivity and economic growth. An extensive body of research shows how these productivity-enhancing investments contribute to boost aggregate output and create new and (sometimes) better jobs. For example, the empirical evidence shows that investments in tangible and intangible assets, innovation, managerial capabilities, and technology adoption are needed to foster the productivity and growth of firms and, therefore, aggregate growth and productivity.[1] The importance of access to finance to fund firms' productive investments is uncontested. Yet, a myriad of distortions and frictions can prevent an efficient allocation of financial resources to firms. In turn, financial constraints hinder firms' ability to make these investments and even use inputs efficiently, thus negatively impacting firms' productivity and growth.

This volume focuses on the links among firm financing, financial constraints, and firm performance, making comprehensive use of firm-level data.[2] It provides, for the first time, a quantitative assessment of the extent of the misallocation of finance, shedding light on the interactions between financial constraints on private firms of different sizes, the role of capital structure, and the impact of such constraints on aggregate growth and productivity. A simple, stylized conceptual framework linking access to finance, firms' performance, and aggregate outcomes, such as growth and productivity, is presented in figure 1.1. This framework can help frame the various discussions in this volume and shed light on the range of factors constraining an efficient allocation of financial resources to firms, thereby hindering economic growth and productivity.

### FIGURE 1.1  Analytical Framework

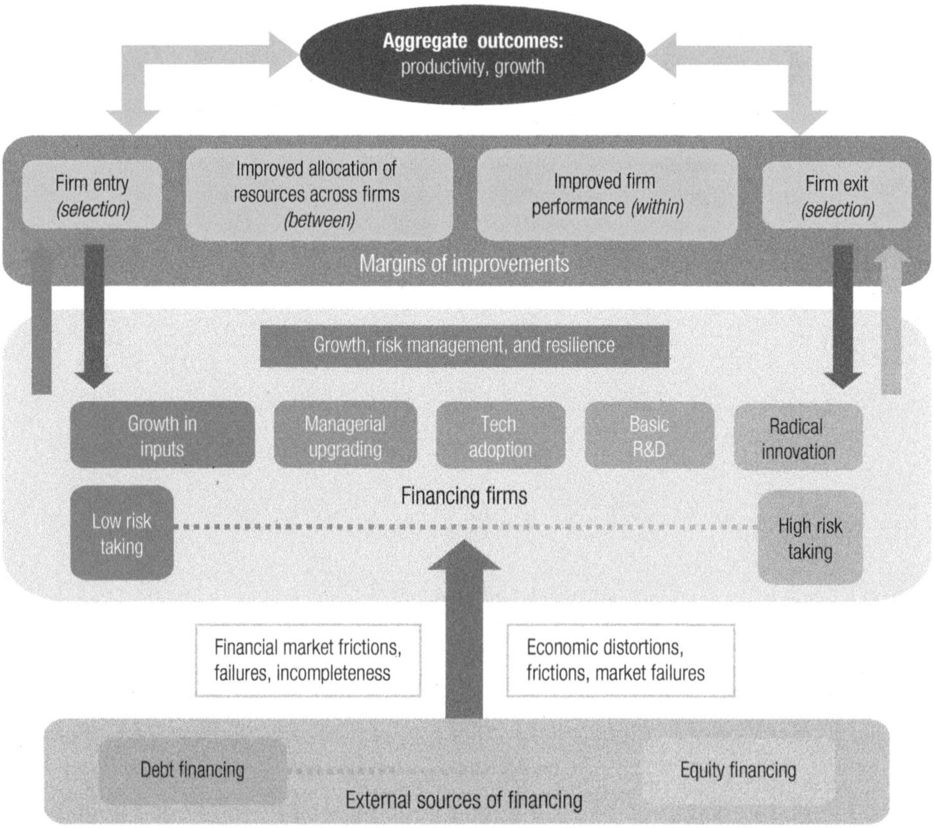

Source: Original figure for this publication, adapted from Cusolito and Maloney (2018).
Note: R&D = research and development.

Access to finance supports firms' performance along three margins: improved performance within the firm (the *within* margin), improved allocation of resources across firms (the *between* margin), and improved dynamics of the entry and exit of firms (the *selection* margin).[3] The within margin captures choices and activities by individual firms to become more productive and improve their performance by innovating, adopting new technologies, or upgrading managerial and workforce skills. The between margin is associated with the reallocation of factors of production and economic activity toward more efficient firms. For instance, the entry of firms with high levels of productivity (relative to the industry average) and the exit of low productivity firms (again, relative to the industry average) can lead to higher aggregate productivity and growth. This selection component thus also reflects the extent to which economic activity shifts toward more efficient firms. Examining the factors that affect the entry of higher-quality firms moves into the study of entrepreneurship.

Hence, firm dynamics lie at the core of aggregate productivity and growth. Firms (and the private sector as a whole) can grow productively in two ways. First, they can increase factor accumulation (such as capital and labor). Second, they can improve their technologies (broadly defined), through technology adoption (process innovation, quality upgrading, managerial approaches, and adoption of new technologies) or through radical (creative) innovation (developments that push the market and global knowledge frontier forward, for instance, by patenting new designs, technologies, and products). The degree of risk taking varies across these different growth strategies. For instance, firm strategies to promote growth by increasing inputs entail the lowest risks, while those through radical innovation entail the highest risks. Firms can also grow by engaging in unproductive entrepreneurship, such as that involving uncompetitive, rent-seeking behavior (such as cartels, lobbying, tax evasion, and lawsuits), various forms of corruption, or illegal pursuits, among others.[4]

Financing and investment decisions are closely intertwined. To the extent that access to finance shapes firms' investment decisions, it will also affect aggregate productivity and growth along the three margins discussed. But how do firms finance their growth? Firms can fund their expansions through internally generated funds or by raising external capital. The latter can take the form of debt or equity financing, including a wide range of hybrid instruments in between. Firms can also turn to other complementary financial products, such as insurance. The mix between financing sources is generally referred to as the firm's *capital structure*. It is important to note that firms' financial needs change according to their ability to generate cash, their growth opportunities, and the risks in realizing them.

This composition of financing sources is an important aspect underlying firms' productivity and growth dynamics. In theory, as Modigliani and Miller (1958) argue, in a world with complete and frictionless markets, firms' capital structure would be irrelevant and would not affect the availability of capital. In the real world, financial frictions, market failures, and market incompleteness abound. Financial frictions—caused, for instance, by informational asymmetries[5] between firms and investors or conflicts of interest—can hinder access to various forms of finance and constrain the ways firms fund their investment projects.[6] In fact, they can lead to underinvestment and alter the investment composition.[7] To the extent that these frictions can be mitigated (or exacerbated) by the choice of contracts between firms and investors (notably, equity versus debt), the type of financing can matter a great deal.[8] Access to different types of financing can thus affect firms' ability to pursue certain expansions. The misallocation of capital, both within and across firms, can have potentially large effects on aggregate outcomes, such as productivity and growth.[9]

*The within margin.* Consider first the within margin and firms' decisions to innovate and adopt technology. How do financial frictions affect firms' undertakings and what are the impacts on firm performance? Innovative activities are inherently risky and generally entail investments in intangible assets (such as research and development (R&D)) that have limited collateral value, due to difficulties in gauging their proper financial value and the high transaction costs in dealing with them. Various studies have argued that equity financing, rather than debt, is a more adequate instrument for funding such types of risky activities, especially at the early stages of the innovation project life cycle.[10] Equity contracts do not require collateral and investors directly benefit when the firm succeeds. This suggests that equity investors, including angel investors and venture capitalists, should be more prominent in industries where investments in intangible assets are relatively large and informational concerns are severe, and less prominent in less innovative start-ups. The latter can also be risky, in that their returns can vary greatly, but they are relatively easy to monitor by conventional financial intermediaries such as banks, suggesting that these activities could be funded through debt.

Corporate financing decisions are often driven by what type of finance is available. Limited access to equity financing may restrict the undertaking of innovative activities. Viable, profitable investments may thus be left underfunded or altogether unfunded. Financial constraints may prompt firms to sacrifice performance to facilitate future financing. For instance, to the extent that the value of a firm's underlying collateral imposes a limit on its ability to borrow through debt, debt-constrained firms would have incentives to distort investments to more pledgeable assets that could be used to secure financing for future investments, thereby alleviating future financial constraints. The financing of innovation, which often entails investments in intangible assets, can be severely affected by financial constraints.

Financial choices are driven not only by investment decisions; they also have a fundamental connection with risk management issues. In theory, firms engage in risk management because financing constraints and incomplete insurance make them effectively risk averse. This behavior renders financial flexibility valuable. That is, it can be valuable for firms to choose a financing mix that preserves the flexibility to respond to future unexpected financial shocks, even at the cost of worse performance, including slower growth. This can be particularly important in countries with significant macroeconomic risks (related to weak macroeconomic fundamentals, such as aggregate instability and low growth, high inflation, high interest rates, high political risks, or high exchange rate risks, among others).[11] For instance, firms may accumulate and hold cash as a buffer. Firms may also use several forms of financing simultaneously (thus having "spare tires") to diversify refinancing risks associated with the dynamics of a single financing source.[12]

*The between margin.* Financial frictions can have an impact on the between margin. Impacts can vary across firms with different attributes, such as firm size and age.[13] For instance, principal-agent problems associated with information asymmetry are more acute for small and medium enterprises (SMEs) than for large firms.[14] At the core of these frictions is the greater opacity of smaller firms. For example, SMEs tend to lack reliable financial statements. SMEs tend to be risky and have high entry and exit rates, partly reflecting lower capabilities. They also tend to lack tangible assets that can be used as collateral. As a result, financiers have greater difficulties in assessing their prospects and creditworthiness, monitoring their actions, and enforcing contractual obligations such as repayment, which can directly affect financing to these firms. A key open question in the literature addressed in this volume is the extent to which inefficiencies in the allocation of financing across firms, emerging from financial frictions and distortions induced by firm size and age, have a sizable impact on aggregate outcomes.

*The selection margin.* Financial frictions can also affect the selection margin through the entry-exit dynamics, as well as the process of creative destruction associated with firm churning. Consider for instance the survival of less productive, highly indebted firms in a given industry. The presence of these so-called "zombie firms" can reduce aggregate productivity growth through three main channels. First, zombie firms themselves exhibit low levels of productivity when compared to the average of the industry, and they crowd out real resources (such as labor and capital) from more productive firms. Second, zombie firms crowd out investments of productive firms (undermining their productivity growth). Third, zombie firms hinder an efficient resource allocation by discouraging or congesting entry of higher productivity firms. They can thus crowd out credit to healthier and more productive firms, thereby preventing them from gaining market share. They can also limit the room for new firms to experiment with promising but uncertain technologies and business practices—further reducing the scope for within-firm productivity gains.

To date, most of the evidence exploring firms' capital structure, investments, and performance (including growth and productivity) has been derived from the experience of high-income countries (HICs), focusing mostly on well-established, large publicly held firms.[15] However, recent research in corporate finance provides some evidence that publicly listed firms are very different from nonlisted, private ones. First, firms listed in stock markets (referred to as publicly listed firms) have better access to capital markets, particularly equity financing. Second, they are less prone to information asymmetries, even when controlling for firm size, partly because of the disclosure and reporting requirements associated with listing on a stock exchange, and have greater coverage by analysts. Hence, the capital structure as well as the size and age profiles of private firms can be different from those of publicly listed firms.

While a few papers have explored the effects of financial frictions or distortions on the growth and productivity dynamics of privately held firms in HICs, much less work has been conducted in the context of emerging market and developing economies (EMDEs).[16] This knowledge gap is relevant because it is difficult to extrapolate the results for HICs directly to the realities of countries with lower levels of financial and economic development.[17] Although many of the issues faced by firms in EMDEs (such as information asymmetries and principal-agent issues) are well captured in the corporate finance literature, the severity of these problems tends to be greater in these countries. Whether and how frictions and distortions may affect firm behavior and market dynamics in ways not often observed by researchers studying publicly listed firms in HICs is thus mostly an empirical question.

The empirical evidence presented in this volume draws primarily on a newly constructed data set of 2.5 million private firms in more than 90 middle-income countries (MICs) and HICs.[18] It provides a quantitative assessment of the extent of financial constraints across private firms and the impact on firm performance and, consequently, on aggregate outcomes, such as productivity and growth. Ideally, this analysis would cover the entire developed and developing world. However, data on firm financials is limited to a selected set of MICs and HICs. Yet, these data allow the analysis presented here for the first time to take a consistent, global view of several long-standing questions in the literature. These include the extent to which inefficiencies in financial markets constrain private firms and the importance of financial constraints in the allocation of resources across firms and in allowing existing firms to expand, improve, and cope with shocks. The volume also sheds light on how these relationships may vary with firm attributes such as firm size and age. Importantly, the analysis explores the ways in which not only the level, but also the composition of financing sources is an important aspect underlying firms' performance. This distinction across different sources of financing can be particularly important for the financing of high-risk activities, including innovation, which constitutes an important channel linking finance to productivity and growth. The volume explores these overarching themes.

The rest of the volume is organized as follows. Chapters 2 and 3 set the stage by establishing where the largest financing gaps are for private firms in EMDEs. While theoretical research indicates that firms' need for and access to finance varies substantially with age and size, there is little empirical evidence on how firms finance their investments, especially in EMDEs. To explore this topic in EMDEs, HICs are used as benchmarks. Chapter 2 explores differences in constraints on debt financing across firms with different attributes, such as firm size and age. The results quantify the so-called "SME financing gap" and highlight that firm size is an effective proxy for firms' financial constraints in MICs.

Chapter 3 focuses on constraints in equity financing, especially for the financing of innovative activities. The results show that there is also a critical financing gap for small private firms undertaking innovative activities. These firms have constrained access to both debt financing and equity financing, which hampers the financing of innovation. The chapter also discusses the role of demand and supply factors in fostering or hindering the development of equity markets in EMDEs. The results show that private markets for equity financing in EMDEs are significantly underdeveloped, and they tend to be concentrated in financing relatively large firms, which constrains the availability of equity financing for smaller, innovative firms.

The volume then goes one step further and shows that these financial constraints on firms in MICs reflect inefficiencies in the allocation of capital and have sizable impacts on aggregate outcomes. To the extent that these differences in firm financing between MICs and HICs reflect financial frictions and distortions and a misallocation of capital, mitigating these frictions and distortions, and thereby relaxing financial constraints, would improve firm dynamics and consequently aggregate outcomes. To shed light on the mechanisms through which access to finance supports firms' productivity and growth in EMDEs, the volume provides novel evidence supporting this hypothesis along two margins: improved firm performance (the within margin), and improved allocation of resources across firms (the between margin).

Chapter 4 explores the within margin. Although the literature has shown positive links between financial market development and national growth rates, it does not necessarily imply that firms use financing to increase their productive capabilities—human capital, physical capital, and intangible capital—and grow. The few studies that have explored these issues for firms in EMDEs use aggregate country- or industry-level data. This chapter explores firm-level data to characterize the direct linkages between capital market financing, its composition (debt versus equity financing), the composition of firms' subsequent investments, and firm growth across a wide array of countries. The chapter provides evidence that financial constraints have a significant impact on firm growth. The results indicate that capital market financing allows firms, especially smaller firms, to relax their financial constraints and realize expected growth opportunities by expanding their productive capabilities. The analysis also suggests that debt and equity markets play important but distinct roles in supporting firms' investments in productive capabilities and growth.

Chapter 5 focuses on the between margin. It analyzes the economic effects of the misallocation of finance for a sample of MICs and HICs, quantifying the aggregate productivity gains countries can obtain by removing financial frictions and distortions.

The results show that relaxing firms' financial constraints, especially for smaller firms, could significantly boost countries' productivity, with the largest gains observed among MICs with lower gross domestic product per capita. The chapter also shows that most of these gains are explained by limitations to access to finance—a level effect—instead of the mix of the types of financing (for example, the mix of debt and equity financing). Lastly, the chapter briefly explores the selection margin by discussing the prevalence of zombie firms and the role of weak insolvency systems in hindering a more efficient allocation of capital and labor.

Chapter 6 explores how financial constraints can constrain firms' ability to cope with adverse shocks. The chapter focuses on the misallocation of finance during the COVID-19 pandemic by examining whether firms that had access to finance were in a better position to overcome the pandemic shock compared to those that were financially constrained. The results show that this was indeed the case. For example, small firms in EMDEs were particularly vulnerable to the economic repercussions imposed by the pandemic, at least in part due to their limited access to finance in the first place. The chapter also provides evidence that policy support provided early on during the pandemic, aimed at mitigating firms' liquidity problems, was not as effective as expected in reaching financially constrained firms.

Chapter 7 concludes with a discussion of the role of policies in unlocking the constraints on firm financing to boost productivity and growth. The analyses in this volume indicate that in EMDEs, size-related inefficiencies in financial markets, which render smaller firms more financially constrained than larger firms and firms of comparable size in HICs, have sizable effects on aggregate productivity and growth. The evidence also highlights the relevance of the composition of financing sources—namely, debt versus equity—for productivity and growth in EMDEs. The original results in this volume thus have important implications for a range of financial sector policy interventions aimed at addressing the financing gaps for firms, especially SMEs, in EMDEs.

## Notes

1. Recent theoretical work has emphasized the importance of innovation to understand firm dynamics and productivity growth. See, among others, Acemoglu, Akcigit, and Celik (2014); Akcigit and Kerr (2018); and Klette and Kortum (2004). Other volumes in this series have looked at these issues, for example, Cirera and Maloney (2017); Cirera, Comin, and Cruz (2022); and Fuglie et al. (2020).

2. The evidence in this volume is based on several complementary data sets with different country coverages. When needed, the volume specifies the sampling for the analysis.

3. See, for example, Cusolito and Maloney (2018).

4. See also the seminal work by Baumol (1990, 1993) that builds a typology of productive, unproductive, and destructive entrepreneurship. This stylized growth framework does not provide guidance on whether these different growth strategies enhance welfare. Unproductive entrepreneurship activities can still be second-best substitutes for inefficient institutions. See, for example, Douhan and Henrekson (2010).

5. Information asymmetry refers to a situation where one party in a transaction has more information than the other party. This situation can lead to an imbalance of power, as the party with more information may be able to use it to their advantage and exploit the other party. The principal-agent problem is a crucial issue in the financial sector, as it affects the trust and transparency between parties.

6. Whereas financial constraints can affect firms' investments and performance, the causality can go both ways. More efficient firms are more likely to perform better, and hence yield higher returns, in the face of a given level of financial constraints. Their higher returns can act as buffers against the risks of bankruptcy and financial distress, while also relaxing financial constraints in the future.

7. Recent research provides some evidence that easing financial constraints can boost firm investments in physical and human capital as well as research and development and innovation, therefore impacting productivity growth. See, for example, Caggese (2019), Cao (2019), and Levine and Warusawitharana (2021).

8. When financial policy can affect a firm's position in product or input markets, the firm has incentives to set its capital structure strategically to influence the behavior of competitors, customers, or suppliers. See, for example, Hellmann and Puri (2000).

9. See, for example, Andrews, Criscuola, and Menon (2014); Arnold and Flach (2017); Buera, Kaboski, and Shin (2011); Buera and Shin (2013); Cong et al. (2019); D'Erasmo and Moscoso Boedo (2012); Dias, Robalo Marques, and Richmond (2016); Gilchrist, Sim, and Zakrajsek (2013); Gopinath et al. (2017); Kalemli-Ozcan and Sorensen (2016); Larrain and Stumpner (2017); Meza, Pratap, and Urrutia (2019); Midrigan and Xu (2014); and Moll (2014).

10. A relatively small but growing literature focuses on the financing of R&D with equity issues. See, for example, Aghion et al. (2012); Borisova and Brown (2013); Brown and Floros (2012); Brown and Petersen (2009, 2011); Campello and Hackbarth (2012); Duval, Hong, and Timmer (2017); Gompers and Lerner (2001); Kim and Weisbach (2008); Kortum and Lerner (2000); Sasidharan, Lukose, and Komera (2015); and Scellato (2007).

11. Without some form of hedging, firms may be forced to underinvest when severe shocks hit because it is costly or impossible to raise external finance. See, for example, Froot, Scharfstein, and Stein (1993) and a brief review of the literature in Denis (2011).

12. See, for example, Adrian, Colla, and Shin (2013); Becker and Ivashina (2014); Cortina, Didier, and Schmukler (2021); Crouzet (2018); Greenspan (1999); Levine, Lin, and Xie (2016); and Rauh and Sufi (2010).

13. For an analysis of the role of size and age in influencing firm dynamics across a large sample of EMDEs, see Ayyagari, Demirgüç-Kunt, and Maksimovic (2021). The authors, however, do not explicitly analyze the role of finance in this relationship.

14. Principal-agent problems for SME financing can arise due to information asymmetry and conflicts of interest between the SMEs seeking financing and the lenders providing it. Adverse selection is one such type of principal-agent problem. For example, SMEs seeking financing may not always disclose their true financial status and creditworthiness to lenders, which can result in lenders funding less profitable SMEs or lending to SMEs that are riskier than anticipated. Another is moral hazard. For example, after receiving financing, SMEs may take on riskier projects than they would have otherwise, knowing that the lender is taking on some of the risk. This may result in the SME taking on too much debt or investing in projects that are not profitable, which can harm the lender's interests.

15. See, for example, Carpenter and Petersen (2002); Coleman, Cotei, and Farhat (2016); Degryse, de Goeij, and Kappert (2012); and Gregory et al. (2005). One exception is Arellano, Bai, and Zhang (2012), who explore a sample of 27 European countries.

16. Throughout this volume, EMDEs comprise middle-income and low-income countries.

17. Among the exceptions are studies using the World Bank Enterprise Surveys, which focus on a large cross-section of privately held firms' self-assessments to analyze financing constraints and performance. See, for example, Ayyagari, Demirgüç-Kunt, and Maksimovic (2013) and

Beck, Demirgüç-Kunt, and Maksimovic (2005, 2008). However, the Enterprise Surveys arguably undersample micro- and small enterprises (see Li and Rama 2015). Moreover, the Enterprise Surveys use a self-reported perception of financial constraints.

18. A number of the analyses in this volume are based on several complementary data sets with different samples of firms and countries. The core of the empirical evidence in this volume focuses on firms not listed in public stock exchanges, referred to as "private firms" throughout the volume. However, some analyses focus on publicly listed firms only or a combination of both. Similarly, some of the analyses have greater coverage of MICs in Europe, whereas others cover a wider sample of EMDEs. When needed, the volume clearly specifies the sampling for the analysis.

## References

Acemoglu, D., U. Akcigit, and M. A. Celik. 2014. "Young, Restless and Creative: Openness to Disruption and Creative Innovations." NBER Working Paper 19894, National Bureau of Economic Research, Cambridge, MA.

Adrian, T., P. Colla, and H. S. Shin. 2013. "Which Financial Frictions? Parsing Evidence from the Financial Crisis of 2007–09." *NBER Macroeconomics Annual* 27 (1): 159–214.

Aghion, P., P. Askenazy, N. Berman, G. Cette, and L. Eymard. 2012. "Credit Constraints and the Cyclicality of R&D Investment: Evidence from France." *Journal of the European Economic Association* 10: 1001–24.

Akcigit, U., and W. R. Kerr. 2018. "Growth through Heterogeneous Innovations." *Journal of Political Economy* 126 (4): 1374–443.

Andrews, D., C. Criscuolo, and C. Menon. 2014. "Do Resources Flow to Patenting Firms? Cross-Country Evidence from Firm Level Data." OECD Working Paper 1127, Organisation for Economic Co-operation and Development, Paris.

Arellano, C., Y. Bai, and J. Zhang. 2012. "Firm Dynamics and Financial Development." *Journal of Monetary Economics* 59: 533–49.

Arnold, J. M., and L. Flach. 2017. "Who Gains from Better Access to Credit? Credit Reform and Reallocation of Resources." CESifo Working Paper 6677, Center for Economic Studies, Munich, Germany.

Ayyagari, M., A. Demirgüç-Kunt, and V. Maksimovic. 2013. "Financing in Developing Countries." *Handbook of the Economics of Finance*, volume 2A, edited by G. M. Constantinides, M. Harris, and R. M. Stulz, 683–757. North-Holland.

Ayyagari, M., A. Demirgüç-Kunt, and V. Maksimovic. 2021. "Are Large Firms Born or Made? Evidence from Developing Countries." *Small Business Economics* 57: 191–219.

Baumol, W. J. 1990. "Entrepreneurship: Productive, Unproductive, and Destructive." *Journal of Political Economy* 98: 893–921.

Baumol, W. J. 1993. *Entrepreneurship, Management and the Structure of Payoffs*. Cambridge, MA: MIT Press.

Beck, T., A. Demirgüç-Kunt, and V. Maksimovic. 2005. "Financial and Legal Constraints to Growth: Does Firm Size Matter?" *Journal of Finance* 60 (1): 137–77.

Beck, T., A. Demirgüç-Kunt, and V. Maksimovic. 2008. "Financing Patterns around the World: Are Small Firms Different?" *Journal of Financial Economics* 89 (3): 467–87.

Becker, B., and V. Ivashina. 2014. "Cyclicality of Credit Supply: Firm Level Evidence." *Journal of Monetary Economics* 62 (C): 76–93.

Borisova, G., and J. R. Brown. 2013. "R&D Sensitivity to Asset Sale Proceeds: New Evidence on Financing Constraints and Intangible Investment." *Journal of Banking and Finance* 37 (1): 159–73.

Brown, J. R., and I. V. Floros. 2012. "Access to Private Equity and Real Firm Activity: Evidence from PIPEs." *Journal of Corporate Finance* 18 (1): 151–65.

Brown, J. R., and B. C. Petersen. 2009. "Why Has the Investment-Cash Flow Sensitivity Declined So Sharply? Rising R&D and Equity Market Developments." *Journal of Banking and Finance* 33 (5): 971–84.

Brown, J. R., and B. C. Petersen. 2011. "Cash Holdings and R&D Smoothing." *Journal of Corporate Finance* 17 (3): 694–709.

Buera, F., J. Kaboski, and Y. Shin. 2011. "Finance and Development: A Tale of Two Sectors." *American Economic Review* 101: 1964–2002.

Buera, F., and Y. Shin. 2013. "Financial Frictions and the Persistence of History: A Quantitative Exploration." *Journal of Political Economy* 121 (2): 221–72.

Caggese, A. 2019. "Financing Constraints, Radical versus Incremental Innovation, and Aggregate Productivity." *American Economic Journal* 11 (2): 275–309.

Campello, M., and D. Hackbarth. 2012. "The Firm-Level Credit Multiplier." *Journal of Financial Intermediation* 21: 446–72.

Cao, Y. 2019. "Financial Constraints, Innovation Quality, and Growth." World Bank, Washington, DC.

Carpenter, R., and B. Petersen. 2002. "Capital Market Imperfections, High-Tech Investment, and New Equity Financing." *Economic Journal* 112 (477): F54–F72.

Cirera, X., D. Comin, and M. Cruz. 2022. *Bridging the Technological Divide: Technology Adoption by Firms in Developing Countries.* Washington, DC: World Bank.

Cirera, X., and W. F. Maloney. 2017. *The Innovation Paradox: Developing Country Capabilities and the Unrealized Promise of Technological Catch-Up.* Washington, DC: World Bank.

Coleman, S., C. Cotei, and J. Farhat. 2016. "The Debt-Equity Financing Decisions of US Startup Firms." *Journal of Economics and Finance* 40: 105–26.

Cong, L. W., H. Gao, J. Ponticelli, and X. Yang. 2019. "Credit Allocation under Economic Stimulus: Evidence from China." *Review of Financial Studies* 32 (9): 3412–60.

Cortina, J. J., T. Didier, and S. Schmukler. 2021. "Global Corporate Debt during Crises: Implications of Switching Borrowing across Markets." *Journal of International Economics* 131: 103487.

Crouzet, N. 2018. "Aggregate Implications of Corporate Debt Choices." *Review of Economic Studies* 85 (3): 1635–82.

Cusolito, A. P., and W. F. Maloney. 2018. *Productivity Revisited: Shifting Paradigms in Analysis and Policy.* Washington, DC: World Bank.

D'Erasmo, P. N., and H. J. Moscoso Boedo. 2012. "Financial Structure, Informality and Development." *Journal of Monetary Economics* 59 (3): 286–302.

Degryse, H., P. de Goeij, and P. Kappert. 2012. "The Impact of Firm and Industry Characteristics on Small Firms' Capital Structure." *Small Business Economics* 38: 431–47.

Denis, D. J. 2011. "Financial Flexibility and Corporate Liquidity." *Journal of Corporate Finance* 17 (3): 667–74.

Dias, D. A., C. Robalo Marques, and C. Richmond. 2016. "Misallocation and Productivity in the Lead Up to the Eurozone Crisis." *Journal of Macroeconomics* 49: 46–70.

Douhan, R., and M. Henrekson. 2010. "Entrepreneurship and Second-Best Institutions: Going beyond Baumol's Typology." *Journal of Evolutionary Economics* 20: 629–43.

Duval, R., G. Hong, and Y. Timmer. 2017. "Financial Frictions and the Great Productivity Slowdown." IMF Working Paper 17/129, International Monetary Fund, Washington, DC.

Froot, K. A., D. S. Scharfstein, and J. C. Stein. 1993. "Risk Management: Coordinating Corporate Investment and Financing Policies." *Journal of Finance* 48: 1629–58.

Fuglie, K., M. Gautam, A. Goyal, and W. F. Maloney. 2020. *Harvesting Prosperity: Technology and Productivity Growth in Agriculture*. Washington, DC: World Bank.

Gilchrist, S., J. Sim, and E. Zakrajsek. 2013. "Misallocation and Financial Market Frictions: Some Direct Evidence from the Dispersion in Borrowing Costs." *Review of Economic Dynamics* 16: 159–76.

Gompers, P., and J. Lerner. 2001. "The Venture Capital Revolution." *Journal of Economic Perspectives* 15: 45–62.

Gopinath, G., S. Kalemli-Ozcan, L. Karabarbounis, and C. Villegas Sanchez. 2017. "Capital Allocation and Productivity in South Europe." *Quarterly Journal of Economics* 132 (4): 1915–67.

Greenspan, A. 1999. "Do Efficient Financial Markets Mitigate Financial Crises?" Financial Markets Conference of the Federal Reserve Bank of Atlanta.

Gregory, B., M. Rutherford, S. Oswald, and L. Gardiner. 2005. "An Empirical Investigation of the Growth Cycle Theory of Small Firm Financing." *Journal of Small Business Management* 43: 382–92.

Hellmann, T., and M. Puri. 2000. "The Interaction between Product Market and Financing Strategy: The Role of Venture Capital." *Review of Financial Studies* 13 (4): 959–84.

Kalemli-Ozcan, S., and B. E. Sorensen. 2016. "Misallocation, Property Rights, and Access to Finance: Evidence from within and across Africa." In *African Successes, Volume III: Modernization and Development*, edited by S. Edwards, S. Johnson, and D. N. Weil, 183–211. Chicago, IL: University of Chicago Press.

Kim, W., and M. S. Weisbach. 2008. "Motivations for Public Equity Offers: An International Perspective." *Journal of Financial Economics* 87 (2): 281–307.

Klette, T. J., and S. Kortum. 2004. "Innovating Firms and Aggregate Innovation." *Journal of Political Economy* 112 (5): 986–1018.

Kortum, S., and J. Lerner. 2000. "Assessing the Contribution of Venture Capital to Innovation." *Rand Journal of Economics* 31 (4): 674–92.

Larrain, M., and S. Stumpner. 2017. "Capital Account Liberalization and Aggregate Productivity: The Role of Firm Capital Allocation." *Journal of Finance* 72 (4): 1825–58.

Levine, O., and M. Warusawitharana. 2021. "Finance and Productivity Growth: Firm-Level Evidence." *Journal of Monetary Economics* 117: 91–107.

Levine, R., C. Lin, and W. Xie. 2016. "Spare Tire? Stock Markets, Banking Crises, and Economic Recoveries." *Journal of Financial Economics* 120 (1): 81–101.

Li, Y., and M. Rama. 2015. "Firm Dynamics, Productivity Growth, and Job Creation in Developing Countries: The Role of Micro- and Small Enterprises." *World Bank Research Observer* 30: 3–38.

Meza, F., S. Pratap, and C. Urrutia. 2019. "Credit, Misallocation and Productivity Growth: A Disaggregated Analysis." *Review of Economic Dynamics* 34: 61–86.

Midrigan, V., and D. Y. Xu. 2014. "Finance and Misallocation: Evidence from Plant-Level Data." *American Economic Review* 104: 422–58.

Modigliani, F., and M. H. Miller. 1958. "The Cost of Capital, Corporation Finance and the Theory of Investment." *American Economic Review* 48 (3): 261–97.

Moll, B. 2014. "Productivity Losses from Financial Frictions: Can Self-Financing Undo Capital Misallocation?" *American Economic Review* 104 (10): 3186–221.

Rauh, J. D., and A. Sufi. 2010. "Capital Structure and Debt Structure." *Review of Financial Studies* 23 (12): 4242–80.

Sasidharan, S., P. J. Jijo Lukose, and S. Komera. 2015. "Financing Constraints and Investments in R&D: Evidence from Indian Manufacturing Firms." *Quarterly Review of Economics and Finance* 55: 28–39.

Scellato, G. 2007. "Patents, Firm Size and Financial Constraints: An Empirical Analysis for a Panel of Italian Manufacturing Firms." *Cambridge Journal of Economics* 31 (1): 55–76.

# 2. Which Firms Face the Largest Financing Gaps in Middle-Income Countries?

**Key Messages**

- Drawing from a newly constructed data set that contains 2.5 million private firms in more than 90 countries, this chapter provides the first comprehensive, quantitative assessment of the extent of financial constraints across private firms in middle-income countries (MICs) and high-income countries (HICs).

- Smaller private firms—especially those with fewer than 100 employees—face the largest financing gaps in MICs. Although there is no variation in leverage ratios across firms of different sizes in HICs, larger private firms tend to have significantly higher debt-to-assets ratios than smaller firms in MICs. Moreover, there is a sizable differential in the debt-to-assets ratios among smaller private firms in MICs relative to those in HICs, and this differential tends to decline with firm size, with no differences observed among larger private firms.

- The results indicate that firm size is an effective proxy for firms' financial constraints in MICs. The finding of larger financing gaps in smaller firms than in larger firms is consistent with size-induced financial frictions and distortions. Hence, it supports theoretical models of firm and industry dynamics in which borrowing constraints vary as a function of the size of the firm, with leverage ratios varying with firm size in MICs. This interpretation does not necessarily carry over to firms in HICs.

- However, the results cast doubt on firm age as an effective proxy for firms' financial constraints in MICs. Young private firms tend to be more indebted than older, mature firms in both MICs and HICs. This finding implies that entrepreneurs borrow to start their businesses and then pay off their debt while they accumulate (internal) equity as they get older. Although there are marked differences in the levels of the debt-to-assets ratios of young private firms between MICs and HICs, this differential does not shrink significantly as firms mature. These results stand in contrast to the hypothesis of age-induced financial frictions, whereby younger firms would face greater financial constraints than older firms.

- The financing of publicly listed firms in MICs is remarkably similar to that of firms in HICs, yet markedly different from that of private firms. This result indicates that to understand the full scope of the differences in firms' capital structures across countries requires going beyond a study of publicly listed firms.

## Introduction

Theoretical research indicates that firms' need for and access to finance varies substantially with age and size.[1] Yet, there is little empirical evidence on how firms finance their investments, especially in emerging market and developing economies (EMDEs) as most of the evidence is for publicly listed firms or private firms in high-income countries (HICs). The relationship between firms' capital structure and their size and age is a crucial but still unknown input into a range of macro models of firm dynamics with financial frictions, including those studying resource misallocation.

The prevailing yet unproven wisdom for EMDEs, especially in policy circles, is that both firm size and firm age are good predictors of firms' financing constraints.[2] To explore this hypothesis in middle-income countries (MICs), HICs are used as benchmarks.[3] The underlying assumption is that in more financially developed countries, where financial markets tend to be deeper and the enabling environment for firm financing is more developed, financial constraints are less binding for all firms. Hence, cross-country differences in debt and equity financing for otherwise similar firms reflect that financial constraints are relatively more pronounced in MICs than in HICs. For a discussion of the challenges of measuring financial constraints on private firms, see annex 2A.

Drawing from a newly constructed data set that contains 2.5 million firms in more than 90 countries, this chapter provides the first comprehensive, quantitative assessment of the extent of financial constraints across private and publicly listed firms in MICs. The results are reported through stylized facts. The chapter sets the stage for the rest of the volume. Box 2.1 discusses the data set and the sample of firms analyzed.

## Stylized Fact 1. Smaller Private Firms Face the Largest Financing Gaps in MICs

Although there is no variation in leverage ratios across firms of different sizes in HICs, larger private firms tend to have significantly higher debt-to-assets ratios than smaller firms in MICs. Firms' capital structure varies significantly along the firm size distribution for private firms in MICs (figure 2.1). These patterns hold whether firm size is measured by total assets or total number of employees. For example, small private firms in MICs (those with 10 or fewer employees) on average have debt-to-assets ratios (leverage) of about 40 percent, whereas larger private firms (typically those with more than 100 employees) have an average leverage ratio of about 60 percent. In contrast, differences in leverage ratios for private firms of different sizes in HICs are less marked. Compared to MICs, the range of variation in leverage ratios is significantly smaller among firms in HICs—between 60 and 65 percent on average across firms of different sizes. Therefore, there is a sizable differential in debt-to-assets ratios for smaller private firms in MICs relative to firms of similar size in HICs. In other words, the differential in firms' leverage between MICs and HICs tends to decline with firm size, with no differences observed for larger private firms.

These patterns of debt financing across firms are confirmed by firm-level panel regression estimates that account for firm-level characteristics that may impact their usage of financing (see annex 2B). The analysis controls for firm age, asset tangibility to capture the availability of collateral, labor productivity to reflect firms' productivity and growth potential, as well as industry and country fixed effects. The estimation results yield a similar inverted U-shaped relationship between firm leverage and firm size for private firms in MICs and HICs, although the estimated coefficients are significantly smaller for the latter. That is, the regression results imply less variation in leverage across firms of different sizes in HICs than in MICs. However, when the estimations are constrained to the range of variation in firm size observed in the sample of MICs and HICs, the results mirror those shown in figure 2.1.

The equity-to-assets ratio is the converse of these patterns. The ratio is negatively correlated with firm size for private firms in MICs, but there is little observed variation in these ratios across firms of different sizes in HICs.[4] For example, the share of equity

## BOX 2.1

### Sample of Private Firms in MICs and HICs

The findings in this chapter are drawn from a cross-section of more than 2.5 million nonfinancial firms around the world, constructed from Bureau van Dijk's Orbis global data set for 2016.[a] The sample comprises firms not listed in public stock exchanges, referred to as "private firms" throughout this volume, as well as publicly listed firms, referred to as "public firms." Although the final data set includes firms in 91 countries, over 85 percent of the private firms in the sample are in Europe: about 36 percent of the firms are in high-income countries (HICs) in the region (about 935,000 firms) and about 51 percent are in middle-income countries (MICs) in the region (about 1.3 million firms). Another 276,000 firms are in China and Vietnam, with the rest spread across a wide range of MICs. The results are qualitatively robust to the exclusion of countries with a very large sample size.

The sample of firms covers formal firms with three or more employees. The core set of results presented covers firms up to age 26 years—this restriction on firm age was imposed due to a break in reporting for older firms in MICs. However, robustness analyses show that the findings are robust to the inclusion of older firms in the sample. The analyses in this volume focus on four key subsamples of firms: private firms in HICs, private firms in MICs, publicly listed firms in HICs, and publicly listed firms in MICs. Table B2.1.1 provides detailed information on the distribution of firm size and age across these four subsamples.

*(Box continues on the following page.)*

Which Firms Face the Largest Financing Gaps in Middle-Income Countries?

15

## Sample of Private Firms in MICs and HICs *(continued)*

**TABLE B2.1.1   The Sample of Firms, by Firm Size and Firm Age**

### A. Age (years)

| Bin | Private firms | | | | | | Publicly listed firms | | | | | |
|---|---|---|---|---|---|---|---|---|---|---|---|---|
| | High income | | Middle income | | | | High income | | Middle income | | | |
| | Range (years) | No. of firms | Range (years) | No. of firms | | | Range (years) | No. of firms | Range (years) | No. of firms | | |
| 1 | 0 to 2 | 69,506 | 0 to 2 | 219,070 | | | 0 to 2 | 474 | 0 to 2 | 42 | | |
| 2 | 3 to 4 | 102,989 | 3 to 4 | 239,243 | | | 3 to 4 | 504 | 3 to 4 | 171 | | |
| 3 | 5 to 6 | 93,853 | 5 to 6 | 195,541 | | | 5 to 6 | 417 | 5 to 6 | 1,136 | | |
| 4 | 7 to 8 | 83,923 | 7 to 8 | 147,268 | | | 7 to 8 | 404 | 7 to 8 | 1,446 | | |
| 5 | 9 to 10 | 84,505 | 9 to 10 | 145,364 | | | 9 to 10 | 474 | 9 to 10 | 1,432 | | |
| 6 | 11 to 12 | 80,199 | 11 to 12 | 140,922 | | | 11 to 12 | 560 | 11 to 12 | 1,526 | | |
| 7 | 13 to 14 | 72,956 | 13 to 14 | 101,920 | | | 13 to 14 | 469 | 13 to 14 | 1,649 | | |
| 8 | 15 to 16 | 76,211 | 15 to 16 | 78,378 | | | 15 to 16 | 453 | 15 to 16 | 1,470 | | |
| 9 | 17 to 18 | 73,180 | 17 to 18 | 66,261 | | | 17 to 18 | 710 | 17 to 18 | 1,312 | | |
| 10 | 19 to 20 | 65,619 | 19 to 20 | 60,357 | | | 19 to 20 | 489 | 19 to 20 | 1,216 | | |
| 11 | 21 to 22 | 75,055 | 21 to 22 | 51,996 | | | 21 to 22 | 421 | 21 to 22 | 1,015 | | |
| 12 | 23 to 24 | 56,891 | 23 to 24 | 64,793 | | | 23 to 24 | 313 | 23 to 24 | 1,168 | | |
| 13 | 25 to 26 | 52,983 | 25 to 26 | 62,997 | | | 25 to 26 | 296 | 25 to 26 | 993 | | |

*(Table continues on the following page.)*

## Sample of Private Firms in MICs and HICs (continued)

TABLE B2.1.1 The Sample of Firms, by Firm Size and Firm Age (continued)

B. Size, by total assets (US$, thousands)

| | Private firms | | | | Publicly listed firms | | | |
| | High income | | Middle income | | High income | | Middle income | |
| Bin | Range (US$, thousands) | No. of firms | Range (US$, thousands) | No. of firms | Range (US$, thousands) | No. of firms | Range (US$, thousands) | No. of firms |
|---|---|---|---|---|---|---|---|---|
| 1 | 0 to 107 | 98,787 | 0 to 6 | 157,489 | 198 to 10,627 | 599 | 3 to 1,750 | 1,458 |
| 2 | 108 to 203 | 98,787 | 7 to 19 | 157,333 | 10,628 to 24,548 | 598 | 1,751 to 3,513 | 1,458 |
| 3 | 204 to 323 | 98,787 | 20 to 38 | 157,448 | 24,549 to 44,084 | 599 | 3,514 to 5,771 | 1,457 |
| 4 | 324 to 480 | 98,787 | 39 to 63 | 157,374 | 44,085 to 73,564 | 598 | 5,772 to 8,914 | 1,458 |
| 5 | 481 to 702 | 98,787 | 64 to 107 | 157,411 | 73,565 to 122,565 | 598 | 8,915 to 14,024 | 1,457 |
| 6 | 703 to 1,047 | 98,787 | 108 to 178 | 157,415 | 122,566 to 220,954 | 599 | 14,025 to 23,550 | 1,458 |
| 7 | 1,048 to 1,661 | 98,787 | 179 to 313 | 157,407 | 220,955 to 464,275 | 598 | 23,551 to 48,014 | 1,458 |
| 8 | 1,662 to 3,052 | 98,787 | 314 to 629 | 157,412 | 464,276 to 1,123,032 | 599 | 48,015 to 131,302 | 1,457 |
| 9 | 3,053 to 8,391 | 98,787 | 630 to 1,840 | 157,411 | 1,123,033 to 3,374,590 | 598 | 131,303 to 417,313 | 1,458 |
| 10 | 8,392 to 24,187 | 32,929 | 1,841 to 3,343 | 52,470 | 3,374,591 to 5,827,121 | 200 | 417,314 to 710,462 | 486 |
| 11 | 14,188 to 32,577 | 32,929 | 3,344 to 8,839 | 52,470 | 5,827,122 to 12,484,323 | 199 | 710,463 to 1,629,472 | 486 |
| 12 | 32,578 to 251,059,440 | 32,929 | 8,840 to 125,335,416 | 52,470 | 12,484,324 to 332,209,216 | 199 | 1,629,473 to 197,492,720 | 485 |

(Table continues on the following page.)

**BOX 2.1**

## Sample of Private Firms in MICs and HICs *(continued)*

**TABLE B2.1.1  The Sample of Firms, by Firm Size and Firm Age *(continued)***

### C. Size, by Number of Employees

| | Private firms | | | | Publicly listed firms | | | |
| | High income | | Middle income | | High income | | Middle income | |
| Bin | Range (number) | No. of firms | Range (number) | No. of firms | Range (number) | No. of firms | Range (number) | No. of firms |
| --- | --- | --- | --- | --- | --- | --- | --- | --- |
| 1 | 3 | 142,301 | 3 to 4 | 210,206 | 3 to 22 | 600 | 3 to 32 | 1,477 |
| 2 | 4 | 103,098 | 5 | 120,154 | 23 to 53 | 598 | 33 to 60 | 1,489 |
| 3 | 5 | 84,571 | 6 to 8 | 172,860 | 54 to 96 | 613 | 61 to 89 | 1,428 |
| 4 | 6 | 66,692 | 9 to 10 | 129,865 | 97 to 158 | 586 | 90 to 128 | 1,439 |
| 5 | 7 to 8 | 106,398 | 11 to 15 | 166,411 | 159 to 280 | 598 | 129 to 188 | 1,466 |
| 6 | 9 to 11 | 101,655 | 16 to 19 | 148,194 | 281 to 543 | 597 | 189 to 291 | 1,447 |
| 7 | 12 to 15 | 90,751 | 20 to 25 | 175,317 | 544 to 1,175 | 598 | 292 to 504 | 1,462 |
| 8 | 16 to 25 | 101,351 | 26 to 34 | 140,433 | 1,176 to 2,800 | 601 | 505 to 1,053 | 1,454 |
| 9 | 26 to 53 | 92,737 | 35 to 60 | 155,127 | 2,801 to 8,007 | 595 | 1,054 to 2,851 | 1,457 |
| 10 | 54 to 99 | 42,307 | 61 to 99 | 57,487 | 8,008 to 13,000 | 201 | 2,852 to 4,466 | 487 |
| 11 | 100 to 249 | 33,194 | 100 to 249 | 57,906 | 13,001 to 27,000 | 198 | 4,467 to 8,558 | 485 |
| 12 | 250 to 508,757 | 22,815 | 250 to 759,028 | 40,150 | 27,001 to 592,897 | 199 | 8,559 to 508,757 | 485 |

*Source:* Calculations based on Orbis data.

*Note:* The table shows the numbers of private and publicly listed firms for each bracket of the distributions of firm size and age across the four subsamples of firms.

a. The methodology for extracting and cleaning these data is outlined in Cusolito and Didier (2022), Gopinath et al. (2017), and Kalemli-Ozcan et al. (2015). Annex 2B describes the regression analysis undertaken and summary statistics on the sample's cross-country coverage. The final data set was constructed for 2010–16, but limitations on data availability at the panel level for firms constrained a more in-depth time series analysis for private firms.

## FIGURE 2.1 High- and Middle-Income Countries Exhibit Differences in Capital Structure along the Firm Size Distribution

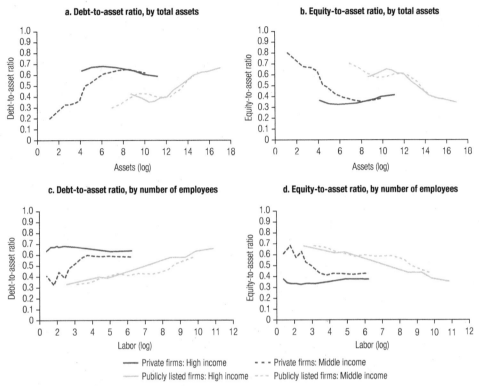

**a. Debt-to-asset ratio, by total assets**

**b. Equity-to-asset ratio, by total assets**

**c. Debt-to-asset ratio, by number of employees**

**d. Equity-to-asset ratio, by number of employees**

—— Private firms: High income          - - - Private firms: Middle income
—— Publicly listed firms: High income   - - - Publicly listed firms: Middle income

*Source:* Calculations based on Orbis data.

in total assets ranges between 42 and 80 percent in MICs and hovers around 40 percent in HICs. Importantly, equity here comprises both internal and external equity. Although data constraints prevent disentangling these two sources of equity, these patterns arguably reflect private firms' usage of internal equity rather than external equity, especially because private equity markets tend to be less developed in MICs than in HICs.[5] Even in the United States, a country with well-developed private equity markets, research indicates that external equity financing plays a small role as a share of firms' external finance (Nanda and Phillips 2022). Access to external equity financing is explored in chapter 3.

These differences in capital structure for firms across countries arguably are related to financial constraints being relatively more pronounced for smaller firms in MICs. In these countries, as smaller private firms grow, financial constraints ease and firms tend to increase their levels of debt financing, thus relying less on equity (especially internal equity). The underlying assumption in this reasoning is that in more financially developed countries, where financial markets tend to be deeper and the enabling environment for firm financing is more developed, financial constraints are less binding for smaller firms. Consistent with this interpretation, Arellano, Bai, and Zhang (2012) show that small firms use disproportionately less debt financing and grow disproportionately faster than large firms in countries with worse credit bureau coverage, larger overhead costs, and lower ratios of private credit to gross domestic product. Therefore, stylized fact 1 is consistent with theoretical models of firm and industry dynamics in which borrowing constraints vary as a function of firm size and thus leverage ratios vary with firm size—for example, as found by Albuquerque and Hopenhayn (2004) and Gopinath et al. (2017). However, the same interpretation does not necessarily carry over to firms in HICs.

## Stylized Fact 2. Young Private Firms Are More Indebted Than Older Firms

In both MICs and HICs, private firms have higher leverage ratios, and hence lower equity-to-assets ratios, when they are younger than when they are older (figure 2.2). In the sample of HICs, young firms (0–4 years) have average debt-to-assets ratios around 80 percent, whereas older firms (22–26 years) have ratios around 56 percent. Similar patterns have been documented for Italy (La Rocca, La Rocca, and Cariola 2011), the United States (Dinlersoz et al. 2019), and a small set of European countries (Kochen 2022). A similar decline in debt to assets is observed for firms in European MICs: 76 percent for the youngest firms versus 37 percent for the most mature firms in the sample. Although there is some heterogeneity across MICs, this negative correlation is observed across countries in and outside Europe. Regression estimates indicate that this negative correlation between firm age and leverage holds after controlling for relevant firm-level characteristics, including firm size, although it is not statistically significant in some specifications.

**FIGURE 2.2  Capital Structure Varies along the Firm's Life Cycle**

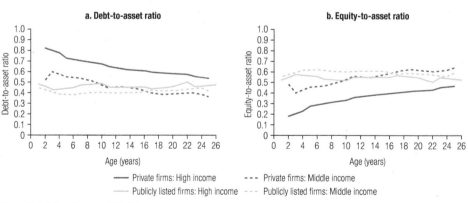

*Source:* Calculations based on Orbis data.

Stylized fact 2 implies that entrepreneurs borrow to start their businesses and then pay off their debt while they accumulate (internal) equity as they get older. This finding is also consistent with start-ups having an inefficiently small scale of business operations. The relative over-indebtedness of younger firms is observed despite the high costs of debt financing for young firms, especially in MICs.[6] Debt is thus an essential source of finance for firms in the initial stages of their life cycles, including those in MICs.

This finding is consistent with corporate finance theories. For instance, the reverse financial life cycle theory predicts that young firms rely on the closest sources of financing—such as borrowing from family and friends and/or bank financing based on family pledges—and firms rebalance their capital structure as they mature.[7] The reputation theory yields a similar prediction—young firms seek credibility by submitting themselves to monitoring by banks.[8] As they age and gain reputation in the marketplace, the signaling effect becomes less relevant and debt levels decline.

Although there are marked differences in the levels of debt-to-assets ratios for young private firms between MICs and HICs, this differential does not shrink significantly with firm age. These results stand in contrast to the hypothesis of age-induced financial frictions, whereby younger firms would face greater financial constraints than older firms. That is, this stylized fact suggests that firm age would not necessarily be an adequate measure of firms' financial constraints across a wide range of MICs. Young private firms are among the most leveraged in MICs, whereas small private firms are the least leveraged.

These results may be related to countries' financial architecture. The patterns of the leverage-age nexus are particularly marked for firms in European countries, which comprise the bulk of the analyzed sample.[9] These countries tend to have bank-based financial systems, with relatively underdeveloped capital markets. In this context, external financing for young firms would more likely come in the form of debt financing, even in the more developed European countries. Consistent with this interpretation, we find that firms in the United Kingdom, a market-based country, have on average smaller debt-to-assets ratios than firms in Portugal, a bank-based country, across the entire age spectrum. However, the evidence for the United States, a market-based country, indicates that leverage and age are negatively correlated, suggesting that there are other factors at play (Dinlersoz et al. 2019).

## Stylized Fact 3. The Capital Structure of Publicly Listed Firms Is Similar in MICs and HICs

Stylized fact 3 indicates that to understand the full scope of the differences in firms' capital structures across countries requires going beyond a study of publicly listed firms. In contrast to the marked differences for private firms discussed above, there are relatively few (if any) cross-country differences in the average debt-to-assets ratios along the firm size and age distributions for publicly listed firms. Debt-to-assets ratios (and equity-to-assets ratios) for publicly listed firms in MICs are remarkably similar to those observed for similarly sized or aged publicly listed firms in HICs.

The capital structure of publicly listed firms is in many ways different from that of private firms. First, the ratio of equity to assets for publicly listed firms is larger than that for private firms of similar size, partly reflecting publicly listed firms' greater access to external equity financing. For example, consider firms with total assets ranging between US$10 million and US$30 million. The equity-to-assets ratio for publicly listed firms averages about 58 percent, whereas the ratio averages 38 percent for private firms. These estimates are of the same order of magnitude for firms in HICs and MICs.

Second, regression estimates indicate that there is a U-shaped pattern in the relationship between leverage and firm size for publicly listed firms, whereas similar regressions show an inverted U-shaped pattern for private firms (see annex 2B). Nonetheless, when these estimates are constrained to the observed size of firms in the sample, the implied relationships between firm size and leverage are similar for public and private firms in MICs. Larger firms tend to have higher debt-to-assets ratios than smaller firms in MICs, independent of their ownership structure. In HICs, leverage ratios are uncorrelated with firm size for private firms, but they tend to increase with firm size for publicly listed firms.

Third, leverage does not vary significantly with firm age for publicly listed firms, in contrast to the negative correlation observed for private firms. Firm-level regression analysis reveals that the estimates for firm age are not statistically significant in the MIC and HIC samples. Once again, an analysis based solely on publicly listed firms would miss the correlation between firm financing and firm age observed in the sample of private firms. Moreover, a similar differential in equity-to-assets ratios between private and publicly listed companies is also observed across the firm age distribution, especially for younger firms. For example, publicly listed firms that are eight years old or younger in HICs have an equity-to-assets ratio around 54 percent, whereas similarly aged private firms have ratios around 24 percent.

## Conclusions

The stylized facts presented in this chapter highlight that firm size is an effective proxy for firms' financial constraints in MICs. To the extent that HICs can be taken as benchmarks, the smaller private firms in MICs—especially those with fewer than 100 employees—face the largest financing gaps. Although there is limited variation in leverage ratios in HICs across private firms of different sizes, there are marked variations across private firms of different sizes in MICs. Smaller private firms tend to have significantly lower leverage ratios than those of larger firms in MICs and firms of similar size in HICs. In contrast, larger private firms in MICs have similar leverage ratios as similarly sized firms in HICs. In other words, the differential between MICs and HICs in firms' leverage tends to decline with firm size, and there is little variation in leverage ratios across countries among larger private firms.

These results thus quantify the so-called "small and medium enterprise (SME) financing gap," which has been an elusive feature in discussions of firms' access to finance. Nonetheless, the statistics presented in this chapter are averages across MICs and HICs and financing gaps can vary in individual countries. A rigorous, data-driven assessment to pinpoint where the most acute gaps are in firm financing and their underlying causes within the context of individual countries is thus crucial, especially for the effectiveness and sustainability of public policies. Chapter 7 will discuss these issues.

The results in this chapter provide support for the notion that financial constraints on firms in MICs reflect size-induced financial frictions and distortions that lead to inefficiencies in the allocation of capital. The findings support theoretical models of firm and industry dynamics in which borrowing constraints vary as a function of firm size, with leverage ratios varying with firm size in MICs. At the core of these financial market inefficiencies is the greater opacity of smaller firms (for example, SMEs tend to lack reliable financial statements), their relatively high riskiness (partly a reflection of lower capabilities), and their lack of assets that can be used as collateral. As a result, for smaller firms, investors and creditors have greater difficulty in assessing the prospects and creditworthiness of these firms in comparison to larger firms, monitoring their actions, and enforcing contractual obligations, all of which can constrain the flow of financing to these firms, especially in the form of debt financing.

The findings in this chapter also indicate that to understand the full scope of firms' financial constraints in MICs requires going beyond the study of publicly listed firms. Publicly listed firms tend to face fewer stringent financial constraints than private firms in MICs. The characteristics of SMEs that set them apart from larger firms tend to be less marked for publicly listed firms. Consistently, the analysis in this chapter shows that the financing of publicly listed firms in MICs is remarkably similar to that in HICs, yet markedly different from that of private firms. Hence, an analysis based solely on publicly listed firms would underestimate the differences between MICs and HICs and miss the negative correlation between firm financing and firm age observed among private firms. The results that are typically documented in the literature on capital structures of private firms in HICs or of publicly listed companies around the world should thus not be extrapolated to the context of private firms in EMDEs.

Lastly, the analysis of capital structures across private firms in different age groups is not conclusive; it casts doubt on the notion that firm age is a suitable proxy for firms' financial constraints in MICs. For instance, the results show that the differential between MICs and HICs in leverage ratios does not decline significantly with firm age,

Which Firms Face the Largest Financing Gaps in Middle-Income Countries?

23

suggesting that younger firms do not necessarily face greater financial constraints than older firms. A potential explanation for these results on firm age lies in the differences between formal and informal firms and the sources of debt financing. The data set explored in this chapter focuses on formal firms with three or more employees. Hence, it does not shed light on the dynamics of firm financing for those that start with fewer than three employees. Moreover, evidence from the early rounds of the World Bank Enterprise Surveys indicates that younger firms rely less on bank financing and more on informal debt financing (Chavis, Klapper, and Love 2011). Therefore, the indebtedness of young firms can still be relatively high, although access to bank finance is constrained. As firms mature, they tend to accumulate more assets and internal equity (thus reducing leverage ratios) and then switch to bank finance. A key question that emerges from these results is how to define financial constraints on firms. Should it capture lack of full access or lack of access to affordable and high-quality financial services? Furthermore, what are the impacts of lack of access to financing and financial constraints on firm investments, productivity, and growth in MICs?[10] Another potential explanation is related to the biases in the coverage of young firms in the Orbis database, a theme that is unexplored in the literature. It is possible that the young firms in the sample are not necessarily small—this could be the case when firms are created as spinoffs, for example. These surprising and somewhat puzzling facts around firm age and financial constraints suggest that further research is needed.

## Annex 2A Measuring Firms' Financial Constraints

Although it is well-accepted that financial constraints can affect corporate investments, the measurement of such financial constraints is challenging and has been the subject of a decades-long, extensive debate in academic and policy circles. This volume aims to characterize the extent of financial constraints on private firms, for which data availability is significantly more challenging than for publicly listed firms. Although the latter are typically subject to mandatory disclosures of their financial statements, no such reporting requirements exist for private firms. Hence, the approach taken in this chapter to measure financial constraints was driven first and foremost by data constraints.

The chapter explored a newly constructed cross-section data set that contains 2.5 million private firms. As highlighted in the text, although time-series financial information is available from 2010 to 2016, the sample size for private firms in MICs is limited. This limited availability of panel data for MIC firms prevents adopting some of the methodologies explored in the relevant financial literature. For example, a large number of studies interpret the sensitivity of investments to cash flows as evidence of financial constraints.[11] The argument is that external financing (be it debt or equity) is not always available when firms are financially constrained. Consequently, the investments of a financially constrained firm would depend heavily on the availability of internal funds (captured by their cash flows). Furthermore, Tobin's Q (measuring the financial market value of firms) is typically evaluated along cash flows. Neither panel data nor market valuations are available for the sample of firms analyzed in this volume.

The World Bank Enterprise Surveys have also been widely explored in the literature. Although these surveys focus on a large sample of private firms in MICs, they measure firms' self-assessments to characterize financial constraints and performance. Moreover, the Enterprise Surveys arguably undersample smaller enterprises. The analysis in this volume relies on actual balance sheet data to quantify the financial constraints on private firms in MICs. The evidence presented here is consistent with that emerging from the Enterprise Surveys—the so-called "SME financing gap," which characterizes stronger financial constraints on SME firms than for larger firms.[12]

The methodology adopted in this chapter benchmarks firms in MICs against those in HICs, interpreting shortfalls in financial structures relative to these benchmarks as evidence of financial constraints. The key underlying assumption is that in HICs, where financial markets tend to be deeper and the enabling environment for firm financing more developed, financial constraints would be less binding for all firms. Hence, cross-country differences in debt and equity financing for otherwise similar firms reflect that financial constraints are relatively more pronounced in MICs than in HICs. The empirical evidence presented in this chapter shows that there is indeed little variation, on average, in leverage ratios across private firms of different sizes in HICs, thus supporting this assumption.

## Annex 2B Regression Estimates

Regression analysis supports the stylized facts documented in this chapter. The following regression specification is estimated using firm-level data:

$$C_{fsc} = \alpha_s + \alpha_c + \beta_1 S_{fsc} + \beta_2 S_{fsc}^2 + \beta_3 A_{fsc} + \beta_4 A_{fsc}^2 + \beta_5 T_{fsc} + \beta_6 P_{fsc} + \varepsilon_{fsc}, \qquad (2B.1)$$

where $f$ refers to firm, $s$ refers to sector, and $c$ refers to country. $C_{fsc}$ is firms' capital structure (measured as the debt-to-assets ratio or equity-to-assets ratio), $S_{fsc}$ is firm size (measured as the log of total assets or the log of the number of employees), $A_{fsc}$ is firm age (based on the year of incorporation), $T_{fsc}$ is asset tangibility (measured as the ratio of tangible fixed assets to total assets), and $P_{fsc}$ is labor productivity (measured as turnover divided by the number of employees).[13] The regressions also include fixed effects at the sector (based on NACE Rev. 2 industry classification) and country levels. The estimation results are reported in table 2B.1. The results are robust to the exclusion of the control variables for asset tangibility and labor productivity.

**TABLE 2B.1  Regression Estimates for Debt-to-Asset Ratios**

| | Private firms | | | Publicly listed firms | |
|---|---|---|---|---|---|
| | HICs (1) | MICs (2) | MICs without large countries (3) | HICs (4) | MICs (5) |
| Independent variables: Firm size | 0.015*** | 0.062*** | 0.029*** | −0.112*** | −0.027*** |
| | (0.001) | (0.000) | (0.001) | (0.012) | (0.007) |
| Firm size squared | −0.001*** | −0.003*** | −0.001*** | 0.005*** | 0.002*** |
| | (0.000) | (0.000) | (0.000) | (0.000) | (0.000) |
| Age | −0.040*** | 0.068*** | 0.002 | −0.025 | −0.055 |
| | (0.002) | (0.002) | (0.004) | (0.020) | (0.034) |
| Age squared | −0.010*** | −0.037*** | −0.021*** | 0.003 | 0.007 |
| | (0.001) | (0.000) | (0.001) | (0.005) | (0.007) |
| Tangibility | 0.078*** | −0.027*** | 0.024*** | 0.159*** | 0.077*** |
| | (0.001) | (0.001) | (0.002) | (0.015) | (0.011) |
| Labor productivity | 0.015*** | 0.041*** | 0.022*** | 0.017*** | 0.025*** |
| | (0.000) | (0.000) | (0.000) | (0.003) | (0.002) |
| Dependent variable mean | 0.617 | 0.484 | 0.488 | 0.461 | 0.417 |
| Dependent variable std. dev. | 0.265 | 0.342 | 0.294 | 0.233 | 0.218 |
| Sector fixed effects | Yes | Yes | Yes | Yes | Yes |
| Country fixed effects | Yes | Yes | Yes | Yes | Yes |
| Observations | 987,870 | 1,574,110 | 553,729 | 5,981 | 14,576 |
| R-squared | 0.191 | 0.211 | 0.137 | 0.197 | 0.123 |

*Source:* Calculations based on Orbis data.

*Note:* HICs = high-income countries; MICs = middle-income countries. Robust standard errors are reported. *, **, and *** indicate statistical significance at the 10, 5, and 1 percent levels, respectively.

## Notes

1. Existing theories explain only certain facets of the diversity and complexity of financing choices. The theories tend to differ in their assumptions about the predominant financial market imperfection that motivates firms' financing structures—such as information asymmetries, distortionary taxation, agency costs, or costly enforcement. See, for example, Albuquerque and Hopenhayn (2004), Cooley and Quadrini (2001), Crouzet and Mehrotra (2020), Khan and Thomas (2013), and reviews of the literature in Caggese (2019), Dinlersoz et al. (2019), and La Rocca, La Rocca, and Cariola (2011).

2. For empirical evidence on HICs, see, for example, Hadlock and Pierce (2010) and Hoberg and Maksimovic (2015) for publicly listed firms in the United States; Dinlersoz et al. (2019) and La Rocca, La Rocca, and Cariola (2011) for private firms in the United States and Italy, respectively; and Arellano, Bai, and Zhang (2012) and Gopinath et al. (2017) for private firms in Europe.

3. Arellano, Bai, and Zhang (2012) and Li and Rama (2015), among others, take similar approaches. Annex 2A provides a brief discussion of the adopted methodology.

4. Peter (2021) provides similar evidence for nine high-income European countries.

5. Over 85 percent of the private firms in the sample have three or fewer shareholders.

6. See, for example, Kochen (2022).

7. See, for example, Hamilton and Fox (1998) and Petersen and Rajan (1994). The seminal papers on this topic are Jensen (1986), Jensen and Meckling (1976), Myers (1984), Myers and Majluf (1984), and, more recently, Dang et al. (2017), focusing on banks versus security markets.

8. See, for example, Diamond (1991).

9. The result that debt is high for younger European firms has been documented in a few other studies of individual European countries and smaller subsamples of European countries (Giannetti 2003; Kochen 2022; La Rocca, La Rocca, and Cariola 2011).

10. A topic that has received little interest in the literature is related to the effect of the quality of financial intermediation on economic performance. Notable exceptions include Hakenes et al. (2015); Hasan, Horvath, and Mares (2018); Hasan, Koetter, and Wedow (2009); and Koetter and Wedow (2010).

11. See, for example, Baker, Stein, and Wurgler (2003); Chen and Chen (2012); Dasgupta, Li, and Dong (2019); Fazzari et al. (1988); Fazzari, Hubbard, and Petersen (1988); Hadlock and Pierce (2010); Hoshi, Kashyap, and Scharfstein (1991); Kaplan and Zingales (1997, 2000); Li (2011); Wang (2022); and Whited (1992) and the references therein.

12. See, for example, Ayyagari, Demirgüç-Kunt, and Maksimovic (2017) and the references therein.

13. This proxy for labor productivity has been used in the academic literature exploring the Orbis database. One of its main advantages is that it does not rely on any assumptions or imputations. Moreover, Gal (2013) shows that this measure allows for the broadest coverage of firms in the Orbis database.

## References

Albuquerque, R., and H. A. Hopenhayn. 2004. "Optimal Lending Contracts and Firm Dynamics." *Review of Economic Studies* 71: 285–315.

Arellano, C., Y. Bai, and J. Zhang. 2012. "Firm Dynamics and Financial Development." *Journal of Monetary Economics* 59: 533–49.

Ayyagari, M., A. Demirgüç-Kunt, and V. Maksimovic. 2017. "SME Finance." Policy Research Working Paper 8241, World Bank, Washington, DC.

Baker, M., J. C. Stein, and J. Wurgler. 2003. "When Does the Market Matter? Stock Prices and the Investment of Equity-Dependent Firms." *Quarterly Journal of Economics* 118 (3): 969–1005.

Caggese, A. 2019. "Financing Constraints, Radical versus Incremental Innovation, and Aggregate Productivity." *American Economic Journal* 11 (2): 275–309.

Chavis, L., L. Klapper, and I. Love. 2011. "The Impact of the Business Environment on Young Firm Financing." *World Bank Economic Review* 25 (3): 486–507.

Chen, H., and S. Chen. 2012. "Investment-Cash Flow Sensitivity Cannot Be a Good Measure of Financial Constraints: Evidence from the Time Series." *Journal of Financial Economics* 103 (2): 393–410.

Cooley, T. F., and V. Quadrini. 2001. "Financial Markets and Firm Dynamics." *American Economic Review* 91: 1286–310.

Crouzet, N., and N. Mehrotra. 2020. "Small and Large Firms over the Business Cycle." *American Economic Review* 110: 3549–601.

Cusolito, A. P., and T. Didier. 2022. "Orbis Database: Methodology and Users' Guide for Cleaning Financial and Ownership Modules." World Bank, Washington, DC.

Dang, T. V., G. Gorton, B. Holmström, and G. Ordoñez. 2017. "Banks as Secret Keepers." *American Economic Review* 107 (4): 1005–29.

Dasgupta, S., E. X. Li, and Y. Dong. 2019. "Inventory Behavior and Financial Constraints: Theory and Evidence." *Review of Financial Studies* 32 (3): 1188–233.

Diamond, D. W. 1991. "Monitoring and Reputation: The Choice between Bank Loans and Directly Placed Debt." *Journal of Political Economy* 99: 689–721.

Dinlersoz, E., S. Kalemli-Özcan, H. Hyatt, and V. Penciakova. 2019. "Leverage over the Firm Life Cycle, Firm Growth, and Aggregate Fluctuations." Working Paper 2019-18, Federal Reserve Bank of Atlanta. https://ssrn.com/abstract=3492473 or http://dx.doi.org/10.29338/wp2019-18.

Fazzari, S., R. G. Hubbard, and B. Petersen. 1988. "Investment, Financing Decisions, and Tax Policy." *American Economic Review* 78 (2): 200–05.

Fazzari, S. M., R. G. Hubbard, B. C. Petersen, A. S. Blinder, and J. M. Poterba. 1988. "Financing Constraints and Corporate Investment." *Brookings Papers on Economic Activity* 1988 (1): 141–206.

Gal, P. 2013. "Measuring Total Factor Productivity at the Firm Level Using OECD-Orbis." OECD Economics Department Working Paper 1049, OECD Publishing, Paris.

Giannetti, M. 2003. "Do Better Institutions Mitigate Agency Problems? Evidence from Corporate Finance Choices." *Journal of Financial and Quantitative Analysis* 38 (1): 185–212.

Gopinath, G., S. Kalemli-Ozcan, L. Karabarbounis, and C. Villegas-Sanchez. 2017. "Capital Allocation and Productivity in South Europe." *Quarterly Journal of Economics* 132 (4): 1915–67.

Hadlock, C. J., and J. R. Pierce. 2010. "New Evidence on Measuring Financial Constraints: Moving beyond the KZ Index." *Review of Financial Studies* 23 (5): 1909–40.

Hakenes, H., I. Hasan, P. Molyneux, and R. Xie. 2015. "Small Banks and Local Economic Development." *Review of Finance* 19 (2): 653–83.

Hamilton, R. T., and M. A. Fox. 1998. "The Financing Preferences of Small Firm Owners." *International Journal of Entrepreneurial Behavior & Research* 4 (3): 239–48.

Hasan, I., R. Horvath, and J. Mares. 2018. "What Type of Finance Matters for Growth? Bayesian Model Averaging Evidence." *World Bank Economic Review* 32 (2): 383–409.

Hasan, I., M. Koetter, and M. Wedow. 2009. "Regional Growth and Finance in Europe: Is There a Quality Effect of Bank Efficiency?" *Journal of Banking & Finance* 33 (8): 1446–53.

Hoberg, G., and V. Maksimovic. 2015. "Redefining Financial Constraints: A Text-Based Analysis." *Review of Financial Studies* 28 (5): 1312–52.

Hoshi, T., A. Kashyap, and D. Scharfstein. 1991. "Corporate Structure, Liquidity, and Investment: Evidence from Japanese Panel Data." *Quarterly Journal of Economics* 106: 33–60.

Jensen, M. 1986. "Agency Costs of Free Cash Flow, Corporate Finance, and Takeovers." *American Economic Review* 76 (2): 323–29.

Jensen, M. C., and W. H. Meckling. 1976. "Theory of the Firm: Managerial Behavior, Agency Costs and Ownership Structure." *Journal of Financial Economics* 3 (4): 305–60.

Kalemli-Ozcan, S., B. Sorensen, C. Villegas-Sanchez, V. Volosovych, and S. Yesiltas. 2015. "How to Construct Nationally Representative Firm Level Data from the Orbis Global Database: New Facts and Aggregate Implications." NBER Working Paper 21558, National Bureau of Economic Research, Cambridge, MA.

Kaplan, S., and L. Zingales. 1997. "Do Financial Constraints Explain Why Investment Is Correlated with Cash Flow?" *Quarterly Journal of Economics* 112: 169–216.

Kaplan, S., and L. Zingales. 2000. "Investment Cash Flow Sensitivities Are Not Valid Measures of Financing Constraints." *Quarterly Journal of Economics* 115 (2): 707–12.

Khan, A., and J. K. Thomas. 2013. "Credit Shocks and Aggregate Fluctuations in an Economy with Production Heterogeneity." *Journal of Political Economy* 121 (6): 1055–107.

Kochen, F. 2022. "Finance over the Life Cycle of Firms." New York: New York University.

Koetter, M., and M. Wedow. 2010. "Finance and Growth in a Bank-Based Economy: Is It Quantity or Quality That Matters?" *Journal of International Money and Finance* 29 (8): 1529–45.

La Rocca, M. M., T. La Rocca, and A. Cariola. 2011. "Capital Structure Decisions during a Firm's Life Cycle." *Small Business Economics* 37: 107–30.

Li, D. 2011. "Financial Constraints, R&D Investment, and Stock Returns." *Review of Financial Studies* 24 (9): 2974–3007.

Li, Y., and M. Rama. 2015. "Firm Dynamics, Productivity Growth, and Job Creation in Developing Countries: The Role of Micro- and Small Enterprises." *World Bank Research Observer* 30: 3–38.

Myers, S. C. 1984. "The Capital Structure Puzzle." *Journal of Finance* 39: 575–92.

Myers, S. C., and N. S. Majluf. 1984. "Corporate Financing and Investment Decisions When Firms Have Information That Investors Do Not Have." *Journal of Financial Economics* 13: 187–221.

Nanda, R., and G. M. Phillips. 2022. "Small Firm Financing Frictions: How Salient Are They and What Are Their Real Effects? Review and Perspectives for New Research." Working Paper 4052767, Tuck School of Business, Hanover, NH.

Peter, A. 2021. "Equity Frictions and Firm Ownership." Institute for International Economic Studies, Stockholm University.

Petersen, M. A., and R. G. Rajan. 1994. "The Benefits of Lending Relationships: Evidence from Small Business Data." *Journal of Finance* 49 (1): 3–37.

Wang, X. 2022. "Financial Liberalization and the Investment-Cash Flow Sensitivity." *Journal of International Financial Markets, Institutions, & Money* 77: 101527.

Whited, T. M. 1992. "Debt, Liquidity Constraints and Corporate Investment: Evidence from Panel Data." *Journal of Finance* 47 (4): 1425–60.

# 3. Financing Innovation

**Key Messages**

- **Innovative activities are particularly challenging to finance with external sources of capital.** They are inherently risky and generally entail investments in intangible assets that provide limited collateral value, due to difficulties in gauging their proper financial value and the high transaction costs in dealing with them. Investments in intangible assets could thus be hard to finance with debt, especially when firms lack other sources of collateral. Equity financing is thus a particularly attractive source of external finance for innovation.

- **The results show a critical financing gap for smaller private firms undertaking innovative activities in middle-income countries (MICs), which hampers the financing of innovation in MICs.** There is limited use of not only debt financing, but also external equity financing among smaller, innovative private firms in MICs, such as high-tech and/or high research and development firms.

- **Private markets for equity financing in emerging market and developing economies (EMDEs) are relatively shallow, and the bulk of the financing goes to relatively large and mature firms, typically in a narrow set of high-tech sectors, such as the software industry.** For example, private firms in MICs with more than 350 employees accounted for roughly 70 percent of the venture capital investments, and firms younger than five years accounted for less than 15 percent during 2010–19.

- **The experience of high-income countries (HICs) indicates that public policies can play a crucial role in closing the equity financing gap.** Policy interventions should aim to tackle the underlying financial frictions and market failures that give rise to the gap in equity financing, while considering the incentives in the marketplace for both firms and private investors.

- **Fostering the development of private markets for equity financing in EMDEs entails tackling a complex set of interrelated demand- and supply-side challenges.** The evidence for a large set of EMDEs points toward deficiencies in the entrepreneurial environment as well as in the enabling environment for equity financing more broadly and the lack of domestic risk capital, both of which are reflected in the underdevelopment of the full spectrum of equity markets, including public markets. A holistic approach to developing the overall landscape for equity financing, entrepreneurship, and innovation would likely improve the prospects for effective policy interventions.

- **Policy makers must also be cognizant of the opportunity costs in allocating resources to support the development of private markets for equity financing, especially when fiscal resources are scarce.** Policy makers need to be realistic about not only the desirability of policy interventions, but also their feasibility and impact, while considering countries' local context. The experience of HICs in developing these private markets for equity financing shows that this is a lengthy and expensive process, marked by design and implementation challenges.

This chapter is based on Didier and Cheuva (2023), a background paper prepared for this volume.

## Introduction

Financing innovation is a potentially important channel that links firms, finance, productivity, and growth. In general, innovative activities are particularly challenging to finance with external sources of capital. Hall (2002) argues that the high-tech sector is the most prone to underinvestment due to financial frictions. Firms typically face two fundamental problems that form the basis for much of corporate finance theory: agency problems and information asymmetries, which are particularly marked for firms raising capital for innovation.

As chapter 1 briefly discussed, innovative activities tend to be inherently risky and generally entail investments in intangible assets, such as research and development (R&D). Such assets are often perceived as a less valuable form of collateral because of difficulties in gauging their proper financial value and the high transaction costs in dealing with them. It is difficult to value intangible assets ex ante and sell them ex post due to limited liquidity and costly redeployment; therefore, intangible assets are generally perceived as riskier than tangible assets. Information asymmetries are particularly acute for innovative firms, exacerbating frictions between lenders and debtors. Hence, intangible assets are often less effective at easing firms' credit constraints. Financially constrained firms that rely on debt have incentives to distort investments toward safer and liquid but potentially less profitable and less innovative projects, due to the high expected costs of external finance in the future. Thus, financial constraints can severely affect the financing of innovation.[1]

A growing body of research argues that equity financing, rather than debt, is more effective at funding innovative projects, firms, and industries.[2,3] Brown, Fazzari, and Petersen (2009) and Brown, Martinsson, and Petersen (2013) find that equity financing has several advantages over debt for funding high-tech investment, especially for young and small firms, due to information problems, skewed and highly uncertain returns, and lack of collateral value. Equity contracts do not require collateral and do not aggravate firms' problems of over-indebtedness and financial distress. Moreover, equity investors directly benefit when the firm succeeds. In contrast, creditors tend to focus on repayment capacity, default probabilities, collateral, and cash flows and share only in downside returns. Hence, they are comparatively wary of funding innovative activities, which are investments characterized by a high probability of failure, but a chance of extremely large upside returns. Consequently, debt financing might be more adequate for tangible investments, whereas equity financing may be more appropriate for funding intangible investments.[4]

Equity markets can thus play a crucial role in supporting high-risk innovative activities, especially private markets catering to private firms that, as shown in chapter 2, typically face larger financing gaps than publicly listed firms. Limited access to equity financing can adversely affect the entry of new enterprises and, conditional on entry, impede the ability of firms to invest in new opportunities and grow. Research has shown that venture capital (VC) not only impacts the performance of its portfolio firms, but also can lead to knowledge spillovers to firms in related fields, with long-lasting impacts on aggregate productivity, innovation, and job creation.[5]

These issues have become particularly important in the wake of the COVID-19 pandemic. As countries chart their path out of the economic repercussions imposed by the pandemic, there has been growing interest in equity financing as an alternative to debt financing. Firms have faced significant financial constraints, especially on taking additional debt financing, as corporate debt levels reach record levels and the risk of over-indebtedness rises, affecting their ability to weather shocks and thrive. Moreover, the exit of firms during the turbulent period of the COVID-19 pandemic has arguably created room for firm entry, thus putting a premium on equity financing to support start-ups. This chapter sheds light on these issues by providing new empirical evidence on the role of private markets for equity financing for start-ups and small firms engaging in innovative activities in emerging market and developing economies (EMDEs). Box 3.1 discusses important definitions for this chapter and the data sources.

**BOX 3.1**

### Definitions and Data

Equity transactions in private markets are those that entail investments in shares and securities that are not traded on a public stock market—that is, investments in private companies. This includes investments in the form of seed investments, venture capital (VC), growth equity, leveraged buyouts, consolidations, mezzanine capital, distressed debt investments, and a variety of hybrids (Lerner et al. 2016).

This chapter distinguishes between two types of equity transactions in private markets: VC and private equity (PE).[a] While both VC and PE investments have the ultimate goal of increasing the value of their targeted companies over time and eventually exiting these investments at a profit, these two types of equity investors have distinct ways of managing their investments and tend to target different types of companies, arguably at different stages of their life cycles.[b] VC investments are primarily risk-taking endeavors, where investors subsidize the negative cash flow of firms early on with the expectation of high future profitability. Firms receiving this type of funding tend to be high-risk, high-return firms. VC can be particularly important for innovative firms, such as those on the technological frontier. These investments are typically made by venture capitalists, but they also include accelerators, incubators, seed and angel investors, and may happen through crowdfunding, among others.[c] In contrast, PE investments focus on improving firms' operational efficiency, for example, by enhancing firm capabilities and imposing greater discipline, so that firms become more profitable (PitchBook 2023).[d] These investments are typically buyouts made by PE firms. Hence, the risk of an unsuccessful exit due to business failure is particularly high for VC transactions compared to PE transactions.

The analysis in this chapter is based on data from PitchBook, a comprehensive database of VC and PE transactions in a large sample of countries from 2010 to 2021. The data set comprises 64 high-income countries, 39 upper-middle-income countries, 37 lower-middle-income countries, and 11 low-income countries.[e] The analysis focuses on completed transactions, excluding failed deals.

*(Box continues on the following page.)*

The final sample comprises about 168,000 firms that received VC funding (about 20 percent in emerging market and developing economies (EMDEs)) and 49,000 firms that received PE funding (about 12 percent in EMDEs).

a. PE transactions comprise buyouts, leveraged buyouts, management buy-in and buyouts, and growth and expansion, among others.
b. PE also resembles VC in other respects, such as sharing similar legal structures, incentive schemes, and range of investors. See, for example, Lerner (2008).
c. Individual private investors using their own money are commonly referred to as angel investors, whereas VC investors are those intermediating the money of others. Building on the work of Hellman, Schure, and Vo (2021), who argue that angel investors and venture capitalists are substitutes, the chapter treats them interchangeably.
d. PE investments have been associated with efficiency gains related to lower levels of employment in targeted companies. For a sample of French firms, Guery et al. (2017) provide evidence of labor shedding effects associated with equity investments in private markets from foreign investors but not domestic ones.
e. See annex 3A for a list of the countries in the sample and Didier and Cheuva (2023) for additional information.

## Underdevelopment of Private Markets for Equity Financing in EMDEs

Private markets for equity financing have expanded considerably over the past decade—from around US$400 billion in 2010 to US$1.85 trillion in 2021. This growth has been particularly marked in middle-income countries (MICs), where annual investments increased more than sixfold, albeit from a relatively low base, reaching US$290 billion in 2021. Despite this growth, private markets remain relatively small in EMDEs, in both absolute and relative terms, when benchmarked against high-income countries (HICs) and public equity markets (figure 3.1). First, private markets for equity financing are smaller in EMDEs than in HICs, and EMDEs with lower gross domestic product (GDP) per capita tend to have smaller markets. In other words, there is a negative correlation between the volume of equity financing from private markets and countries' level of economic development. Second, relative to HICs, private markets for equity financing in EMDEs are relatively more underdeveloped than public equity markets. That is, the differential in market size between HICs and EMDEs is larger for private markets than for public markets. Third, the variation of VC and private equity (PE) market development in EMDEs is an order of magnitude smaller than that in HICs. The vast majority of EMDEs have small VC markets, about 0.1 percent of gross domestic product or less. Only a handful of countries have markets with greater depth.

The underdevelopment of private markets for equity financing in EMDEs is notable in both depth and access. Fewer firms obtain financing from private markets in EMDEs compared to those in HICs (figure 3.2).[6] Even when controlling for country size, the differences are marked: about 1.5 and 0.6 firms per million people received VC and PE investments, respectively, in upper-middle-income countries compared to roughly 29 firms and 7 firms per million people, respectively, in HICs per year on average in 2018–19. Furthermore, the cross-country differences are striking. VC investments did not reach more than 10

## FIGURE 3.1    Depth of Private Markets for Equity Financing, 2018–19

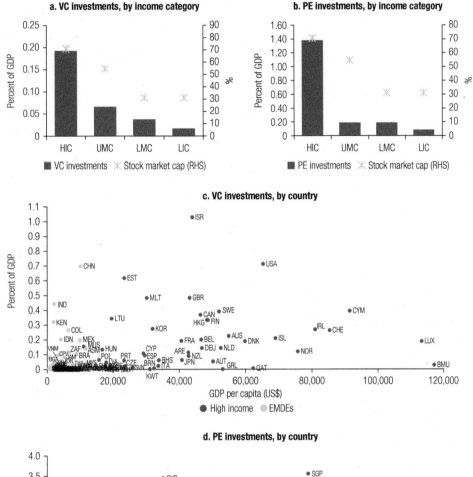

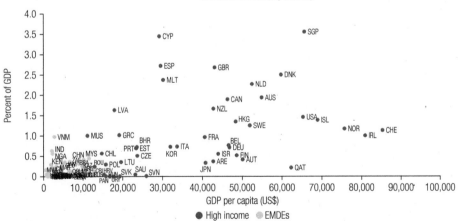

*Source:* Didier and Cheuva 2023.

*Note:* The figure shows the total value of VC and PE investments from deals concluded during 2018–19. Countries are classified according to the World Bank's income classification of countries as of June 2020. The figure uses International Organization for Standardization country codes. EMDEs = emerging market and developing economies; GDP = gross domestic product; HIC = high-income countries; LIC = low-income countries; LMC = lower-middle-income countries; PE = private equity; RHS = right-hand side; UMC = upper-middle-income countries; VC = venture capital.

## FIGURE 3.2 Number of Companies Funded through Private Markets for Equity Financing

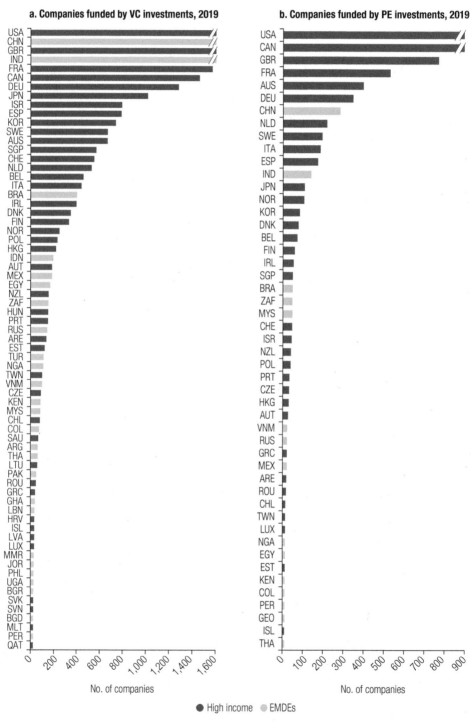

### a. Companies funded by VC investments, 2019

No. of companies

### b. Companies funded by PE investments, 2019

No. of companies

● High income  ● EMDEs

*(Figure continues on the following page.)*

Unleashing Firm Productivity through Firm Financing

**FIGURE 3.2** **Number of Companies Funded through Private Markets for Equity Financing** *(continued)*

**c. Companies funded by VC investments and GDP per capita, 2018–19**

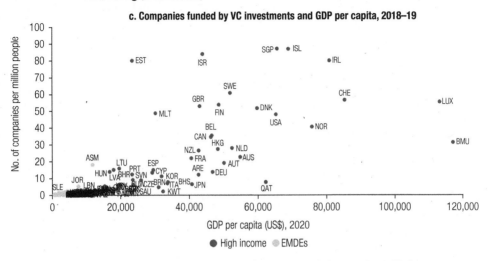

**d. Companies funded by PE investments and GDP per capita, 2018–19**

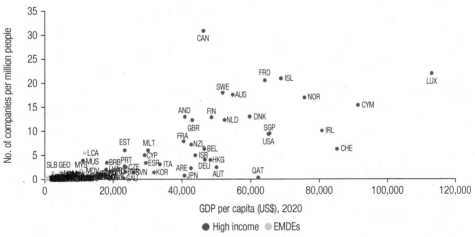

*Source:* Didier and Cheuva 2023.

*Note:* The figure shows the numbers of companies funded through VC and PE investments from deals concluded during 2018–19. Countries are classified according to the World Bank's income classification of countries as of June 2020. The figure uses International Organization for Standardization country codes. EMDEs = emerging market and developing economies; GDP = gross domestic product; PE = private equity; VC = venture capital.

companies per million people in a given year in any EMDE, whereas among the most developed markets in HICs, VC investments reached more than 80 companies per million people. The differences are as stark in PE markets, with transactions reaching at most two companies per million people in EMDEs versus 10 times more in some HICs. Overall, the underdevelopment of VC and PE markets indicates a limited role for private markets for equity financing in supporting firms' productive growth, especially for smaller firms, in EMDEs.[7]

## Equity Financing in Private Markets for High-Tech Firms

There is no such thing as a typical young and small firm. Young and small firms range from "mom and pop" and subsistence operations to high-tech firms, they may be high- or low-growth firms, and so on. An important question is, which of these different young and small firms are equity investors in private markets funding? Equity investors in private markets might have better information and/or better ability to evaluate firm quality compared to other investors, thus dampening the adverse selection and moral hazard problems of entrepreneurial finance. For example, angel investors and venture capitalists should be more active in industries that are prone to a high degree of information asymmetries and associated with large investments in intangible assets (which provide no collateral value for debt financing)—such as biotechnology and computer software, rather than less innovative start-ups, like restaurants and retail outlets. The latter are risky, in that returns show high variance, but it is relatively easy for financial intermediaries offering debt financing to monitor them.

Although economic theory states that equity financing has several advantages over debt for funding investments in risky, innovative activities, equity financing in private markets goes to a relatively narrow set of activities. An analysis of the composition of VC investments, in both HICs and EMDEs, shows that VC funding is concentrated in a narrow set of high-tech sectors.[8] The top-five company verticals across VC investments during 2010–19 were technology, media, and telecommunications; mobile; software as a service; artificial intelligence and machine learning; and e-commerce (figure 3.3).[9] These industries underscore the dominance of the technology sector in VC investments. The top-five verticals accounted for more than 70 percent of the value of VC investments and more than 70 percent of the number of firms that received VC investments not only in HICs, but also in MICs. To the extent that these firms represent a relatively smaller market share of the total economy in MICs compared to HICs, this result shows that the tech industry is overrepresented in VC markets in MICs.

Although these top-five verticals entail high-tech, innovative activities, the uncertainty about the viability and commercialization of ideas can be resolved "quickly," that is, within the time frame of VC investments (Lerner and Nanda 2020). Research highlights that VC funds have a typical timeline of between 8 and 10 years—with 5 years to invest the initial capital raised and the remaining years to exit these investments. Hence, VC investors would look for investment opportunities with gestational periods within this time frame, forgoing those with longer time frames. For example, software-as-a-service businesses are typically based on existing, proven technologies with short development times and can benefit from quick market feedback. In contrast, other innovative, high R&D industries—such as clean energy and new materials, which are less amenable to such rapid learning about their potential demand and would typically have longer gestational periods—account for relatively small shares of VC investments, not only in MICs but even in HICs. In addition, overall industry size and performance (for example, of the high-growth segment) may play an important role in driving these equity investments as they affect not only the risk-return profile of these transactions, but also the exit options for investors.

## FIGURE 3.3  VC and PE Investments across Industries, 2010–19

**a. Top-five company verticals for VC investments**

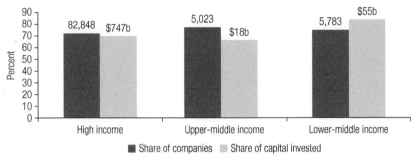

**b. PE investments in the top-three company verticals**

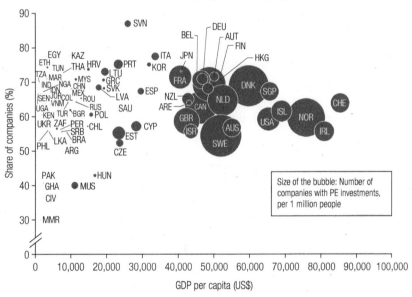

*Source:* Didier and Cheuva 2023.

*Note:* In panel a, the numbers in brackets show the total number of companies and the total financing amount from VC investments within the top-five verticals, which are technology, media, and telecommunications; mobile; software as a service; artificial intelligence and machine learning; and e-commerce. China is excluded from panel a. Panel b shows in the y-axis the share of companies with PE investments in the top three verticals, which are manufacturing, industrials, and oil and gas. The size of the bubble represents the number of companies that received PE investments per 1 million people. The figure uses International Organization for Standardization country codes. GDP = gross domestic product; PE = private equity; VC = venture capital.

This concentration in a relatively narrow set of segments may be privately optimal from the perspective of the investors, but it could have important welfare implications. For instance, even if private markets for equity financing are further developed, they may have a limited role in financing a wider range of innovative investments in EMDEs.

In stark contrast to the composition of VC investments, there is not only significantly more heterogeneity in PE investments, but also greater focus on more traditional sectors. The top verticals for PE investments are manufacturing, industrials, and the oil and gas industry. The average HIC has a share of PE capital invested in companies within these verticals of about 63 percent, whereas the average MIC has a share of 62 percent. Similar statistics are obtained when analyzing the share of companies.

### Debt Financing for High R&D Firms

It could be difficult to finance investments in intangible assets with debt, especially when firms lack other sources of collateral. Evidence from a large cross-section of private and public nonfinancial firms around the world, constructed from the Bureau van Dijk's Orbis global data set discussed in chapter 2, supports this view: high R&D firms tend to have significantly lower leverage ratios, and thus higher equity-to-asset ratios, than other firms (figure 3.4). This is especially so for smaller private firms. Small high R&D firms have lower leverage ratios than small, low R&D firms and large firms. For example, the debt-to-assets ratio of the smallest high R&D private firms in MICs is more than 10 percentage points below that of low R&D private firms in the same size group. Although these differentials decrease with firm size, they persist along the firm age distribution. Interestingly, differences in debt levels between high R&D and low R&D publicly listed firms are less marked than for private firms in MICs. Differences in debt levels for publicly listed firms tend to be larger in HICs compared to the differential for private firms. Importantly, the differential between high R&D and

**FIGURE 3.4  Capital Structure of High R&D Firms**

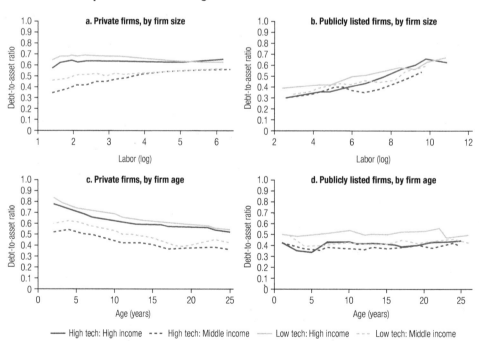

*Source:* Calculations based on Orbis data.

*Note:* This figure excludes two middle-income countries with very large samples of firms, namely, the Russian Federation and Vietnam. The results are qualitatively similar when these two countries are included. R&D = research and development low R&D firms is larger in MICs than in HICs, especially among smaller private firms, indicating that access to debt financing is more challenging for small, innovative firms in MICs.

## Equity Financing for Young and Small Firms

Contrary to popular perception, equity financing plays a minor role in funding the initial stages of innovation in MICs, and even in HICs.[10] VC arguably plays a more prominent role in funding the next stage of the innovation cycle, when companies commercialize their innovation.[11] VC investments have limited reach to start-ups and young firms in MICs. The bulk of the VC investments is concentrated in firms that are five years or older (figure 3.5). The profile of VC investments in MICs is similar to that of HICs, especially in upper-middle-income countries. For example, less than 1 percent of the VC invested

**FIGURE 3.5   VC Investments across Firm Age, 2019**

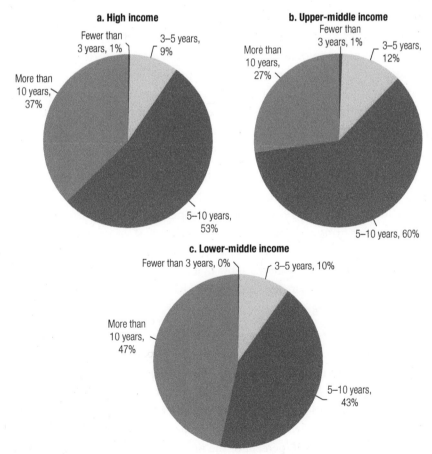

*Source:* Didier and Cheuva 2023.

*Note:* This figure shows the share of capital invested in firms in various age brackets at the time of the investments. China is excluded from the statistics. Data on the foundation year for companies receiving VC funding are available only for 2019. VC = venture capital.

went to firms younger than three years, and less than 12 percent went to firms younger than five years in MICs. Moreover, roughly half of the VC financing in lower-middle-income countries went to firms older than 10 years.

Even when focusing on seed capital—the earliest stage of the capital raising process of a start-up—similar patterns emerge. VC investments have limited reach to firms younger than three years in MICs. For example, in upper-middle-income (lower-middle-income) countries, about 61 (44) percent of seed financing went to firms aged three to five years, whereas about 8 (5) percent went to firms younger than three years. At the other end of the spectrum, PE investments focus primarily on mature firms. In upper-middle-income countries, about 90 percent of PE investments went to firms aged 10 years or more, and another 8 percent went to firms aged 5–10 years. Similar figures are observed in HICs and lower-middle-income countries.

Interestingly, not all young firms that are financed with VC investments are small firms. Some young firms that received VC funding are large and capture a sizable fraction of the funding in MICs. For example, almost 40 percent of the VC investments in firms aged five years or younger went to firms with more than 150 employees in upper-middle-income countries and more than 70 percent in lower-middle-income countries. In contrast, about 24 percent of the VC financing in HICs went to relatively young but large firms. Overall, these patterns indicate that private markets for equity financing in MICs have not focused on funding start-ups; instead, they tend to concentrate on more mature and established firms.

Furthermore, the bulk of the equity financing in private markets in MICs is concentrated on relatively larger firms, more so than in HICs (figure 3.6). For example, private firms with more than 350 employees accounted for roughly 70 percent of the VC investments in MICs during 2010–19, compared to 35 percent in HICs. The differences in VC financing across firms of different sizes are less marked if the comparisons are based on the number of firms, suggesting that a few larger firms capture the bulk of the VC financing in MICs. These patterns show that smaller firms in MICs not only have constrained access to debt financing, as shown in chapter 2, but also have limited access to external equity financing.

Compared to VC investors, PE investors are less likely to fund companies with high risks of business failure. To the extent that smaller firms have more uncertain and skewed returns than larger firms, and hence have a higher probability of failure, PE investors would tend to favor larger firms, compared to VC investors.[12] The analysis indicates that this is indeed the case in both HICs and EMDEs alike. The concentration of investment toward larger firms is even more pronounced for PE investments than for VC investments. More than 50 percent of the firms receiving PE investment in MICs have more than 350 employees, whereas in HICs, about 31 percent of PE investments went to firms with more than 350 employees.

**FIGURE 3.6  Equity Financing in Private Markets across Firm Size, 2010–19**

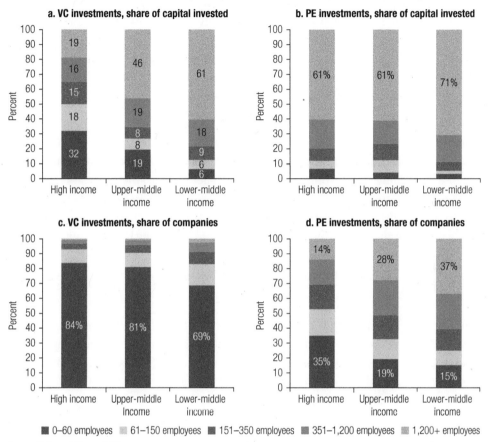

*Source:* Didier and Cheuva 2023.

*Note:* Given the large magnitude of its VC investments and so as not to dwarf the statistics for other upper-middle-income countries, China is excluded from the statistics in panels a and c. PE = private equity; VC = venture capital.

The differences in equity financing in private markets to different sized firms between HICs and MICs can be partly traced to the participation of foreign investors. Foreign investors participated in a large share of the VC investments in MICs during 2010–19—about 58 percent of the total VC investments had foreign investor participation. The average size of foreign investor deals was significantly larger than that of deals involving only domestic investors. For example, VC investments with the participation of investors from HICs were almost double the size of VC transactions with the participation of only domestic investors—US$7.9 million in HICs and US$4.1 million in upper-middle-income countries. In HICs, foreign investors participated in fewer deals (roughly half of the VC transactions) and invested relatively smaller amounts compared to the participation of foreign investors in MICs.

These results suggest that the existence of a robust domestic investor base would be important to expand financing for smaller innovative firms in EMDEs, as foreign investors might not be "perfect substitutes" for domestic investors. The findings are consistent with the idea that foreign investors have less information about local markets and may be more risk averse than domestic investors. Nonetheless, foreign investors could play an important role in developing private markets for equity financing in MICs. Lerner (2013) notes that in most of the entrepreneurial hubs that have emerged over the past two decades, critical early investments were not made by domestic investors, but rather by sophisticated international investors.

The small scale of the private markets in EMDEs explains part of the focus of investments on relatively larger and more mature firms in MICs. Corporate finance theory argues that risk-taking behavior by equity investors is tightly linked to potential payoffs. With a more limited range of investments in smaller markets, the stakes are higher for each individual transaction. Hence, equity investors would have incentives to focus on relatively safer firms, for which demonstration of viability and credibility in the marketplace may have already been established, thereby also enhancing their exit options.

### Demand and Supply Factors Underlying the Underdevelopment of Private Markets for Equity Financing

The key constraints underlying the underdevelopment of private markets for equity financing in EMDEs encompass demand-side factors (such as limited entrepreneurship activity and lack of investment opportunities) and supply-side factors (such as lack of capital and a deficient institutional and regulatory environment for equity financing). Both sets of factors matter. EMDEs tend to underperform compared to HICs on both demand and supply dimensions, although to varying degrees across the developing world, as suggested by the Venture Capital and Private Equity Attractiveness Index (figure 3.7, panel a).[13]

On the supply side, exit conditions are crucial for equity financing in private markets. Since most small and young firms initially do not generate enough profits to pay dividends or buy back shares, the exit route is the primary way that venture capitalists can realize positive returns on their investments. Equity investors can exit from their investments in private markets in multiple ways: the firm can fail (for example, bankruptcy), the firm can be acquired by another firm (strategic exit), the firm can be sold to another investor or bought by those in the firm itself (buyout and buyback exits), or the firm can go public via initial public offering (IPO).[14]

A popular perception is that IPOs constitute the main exit route for equity investors in private markets. In this case, the underdevelopment of public markets would hinder private market development. Although VC-backed firms may represent a large share of IPOs, IPOs account for a small fraction of VC and PE exits, even in countries with well-developed markets such as the United States.[15] On average, IPOs represent about 12 percent of the exits from equity investments in private markets in HICs and upper-middle-income countries.[16] Research indicates that IPOs are typically limited to the most innovative and promising ventures.[17] The vast majority of equity investors in

## FIGURE 3.7   Equity Financing in Private Markets across Firm Size

### a. Venture Capital and Private Equity Attractiveness Index, 2021

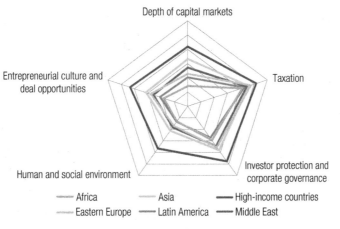

### b. An example of the interplay between demand and supply factors, 2018–19

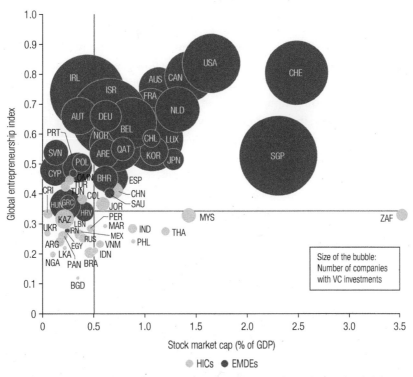

*Sources:* For panel a, calculations are based on data from the IESE Business School; for panel b, calculations are based on data from the World Development Indicators, PitchBook, Global Entrepreneurship and Development Institute, and Didier and Cheuva 2023.

*Note:* In panel b, the size of the bubble represents the number of companies that received VC investments. The green lines show the median values across countries of the stock market capitalization, in the x-axis, and global entrepreneurship index, in the y-axis. The figure uses International Organization for Standardization country codes. EMDEs = emerging market and developing economies; GDP = gross domestic product; HICs = high-income countries; VC = venture capital.

private markets need alternative exit options. Botelho, Fehder, and Hochberg (2021) highlight that the understanding of non-IPO exits constitutes an important knowledge gap, largely unexplored in the literature, even for HICs.

Public equity market development may be a proxy for a range of needed preconditions for private market development. Countries with underdeveloped public equity markets rarely have well-developed private markets. However, countries with well-developed private markets for equity financing tend to have well-developed public equity markets (figure 3.7, panel b). Hence, the underdevelopment of private and public equity markets in a large set of MICs points toward challenges in the development of equity markets more broadly: riskiness, as projects may be too risky for private investors in local markets; a shallow investor base, with too few and small institutional investors, especially domestic ones; and deficiencies in the enabling environment around equity financing, including information asymmetries and limited investor protection (especially for minority share-holders in private companies) as well as corporate governance issues.[18] Yet, public equity market development does not constitute a "sufficient condition" for private market development. A number of MICs have deep and inclusive stock markets but relatively under-developed private markets for equity financing.

The organizational structure of the equity industry in private markets, which ultimately shapes incentives for investors, also affects the flow of equity capital toward innovative firms. The concentration of VC in a narrow set of industries can be interpreted as a financial friction, leading to a shortage of funding for innovative projects in other industries. More broadly, the literature on private market development in HICs provides robust evidence of the impact on the capital allocation of a wide range of financial frictions associated with the organizational structure of the equity industry in private markets—from staged financing and coordination frictions to concentration of capital in a few investors, to the short time horizon of investment rounds and the remuneration structure for venture capitalists and portfolio managers.[19]

Although much attention has been devoted to the challenges in expanding the supply of equity finance for innovative firms, the lack of firms' readiness to receive equity investment can also play a role, affecting the effectiveness of potential interventions supporting equity market development. Investors typically perceive these constraints as limited investment opportunities or limited deal flow. Indeed, the literature shows that important constraints stem from firms themselves (the demand side)—for example, the lack of readiness of firms to receive equity investments.[20] Innovative firms in EMDEs often find it challenging to transform their creative ideas into a viable business proposition, thereby allowing them to attract external funding to develop and commercialize their inventions. Mason and Kwok (2010) highlight three main aspects of this lack of readiness. First, many entrepreneurs may be equity averse, unwilling to surrender ownership and control of their firms. Second, external investors consider that many businesses that seek external finance are not invest-ible, due to deficiencies in their managerial structure, marketing strategy, financial accounts, intellectual property protection, and other business areas. Third, even if entrepreneurs were willing to consider equity and had investible projects, presentational failings mean that many firms are unable to pitch their ideas successfully to investors.

Figure 3.7, panel b, illustrates the interplay between demand and supply factors. Countries with high scores on the Global Entrepreneurship Index (GEI)—which captures a country's entrepreneurial environment, including entrepreneurial attitudes, abilities, and aspirations—and deep capital markets tend to have relatively large VC markets. Analogously, in countries that perform poorly on both fronts, relatively few firms receive VC investments. Akin to the high-level assessment of supply-side factors, the evidence also indicates that a well-developed entrepreneurship environment is a "necessary but not sufficient" condition for the development of private markets for equity financing. No country with a GEI value below the median has a well-developed VC market. However, several countries score relatively high on the GEI but do not have VC markets with significant outreach.

## Conclusions

The evidence in this chapter indicates that there is a critical financing gap for small private firms undertaking innovative activities in MICs. These firms have constrained access to external debt financing and limited access to external equity financing. Private markets for equity financing in EMDEs more broadly are underdeveloped and have limited reach, suggesting that the equity financing gap is likely observed across a wider set of EMDEs. They play a limited role in advancing substantial technological change as the bulk of equity investments through private markets is concentrated on relatively larger and mature firms, and in the case of VC, typically in a narrow set of high-tech sectors, such as the software industry. In other words, the equity financing gap for private firms is acute for the smaller and innovative firms in a country. Because equity financing can be particularly effective in financing innovation, at least for a subset of firms, the equity financing gap can have significant aggregate economic implications, including for the extent of innovation in EMDEs. These are topics explored in the next chapters.

The experience of HICs indicates that public policies can play a crucial role in closing the equity financing gap. Given the underdevelopment of private markets for equity financing in EMDEs, policy makers should place significant emphasis on market creation when deploying support. But developing such markets for equity financing—comprising the full spectrum of equity markets, from seed and angel investors to VC and PE markets—through government programs presents substantial design challenges, which can doom a program from its start, and implementation challenges, which can create problems as programs enter operation. For instance, Lerner (2013) points to distortions to or absence of incentives, especially for private investors; the size of programs, sometimes too small, sometimes too large; the absence of appropriate evaluation mechanisms; and programs that ignore the international nature of the entrepreneurial process. In addition, the experience of HICs indicates that interventions supporting equity market development would likely require a longer time horizon to reach sustained impact. Hence, policy makers should be prepared to provide patient capital.

Although the empirical evidence is limited, the experience of HICs, along with the results in this chapter, also suggests that policy interventions to support equity market development are more likely to succeed when certain preconditions are in place. Among these preconditions are the existence of a strong institutional investor base (especially comprised of domestic institutional investors) and a well-developed entrepreneurial environment. In other words, policy makers need to take into account countries' local context. Policy interventions should aim to tackle the specific financial frictions and market failures that give rise to the gaps in access to equity financing in individual countries, while considering the incentives in the marketplace for both firms and private investors. In this context, policy targeting tailored to individual country contexts is critical to ensure that scarce funding reaches those that would benefit the most from equity financing. For this, access to granular data and more research would be important, especially in EMDEs. Chapter 7 returns to this discussion.

In EMDEs, fostering the development of private markets for equity financing entails tackling a complex set of interrelated demand- and supply-side challenges. Although this chapter did not provide an in-depth analysis of specific challenges, the evidence presented here for a large set of EMDEs suggests that among these challenges are deficiencies in the entrepreneurial environment as well as in the broader enabling environment for equity financing and the lack of domestic risk capital. These challenges are reflected in the underdevelopment of the full spectrum of equity markets, including public markets. Hence, financial sector policies alone may not be enough to support the development of private markets for equity financing and close the equity financing gap for smaller, innovative firms in EMDEs. A holistic approach to developing the overall landscape for equity financing, entrepreneurship, and innovation would likely improve the prospects for effective policy interventions.

Research on the effectiveness of specific government policies supporting the financing of innovation and the development of equity markets, especially private markets, remains scarce. For instance, there has been no systematic evaluation of the costs of government intervention in supporting private market development, even in HICs. There is also limited evidence on when and how government interventions should occur—for example, the most effective form of ownership structure for government sponsored VC funds. At the core of this lack of research is lack of data. Although information is typically available for entrepreneurs who have obtained (private and public) equity financing with or without government support, information on the counterfactual, that is, those who did not get equity financing, is often missing. More research is needed in this area, especially on the effectiveness of interactions among different government policies, such as between initiatives supporting the development of private markets for equity financing and those fostering entrepreneurial activities.

# Annex 3A Sample of Economies

| Private Equity Markets: Sample of Economies | | | | | | |
|---|---|---|---|---|---|---|
| **High-income** | | **Upper-middle-income** | | **Lower-middle-income** | | **Low-income** |
| 1 Andorra | 33 Japan | 1 American Samoa | 33 Peru | 1 Algeria | 33 Uzbekistan | 1 Burkina Faso |
| 2 Australia | 34 Korea, Rep. | 2 Argentina | 34 Russian Federation | 2 Bangladesh | 34 Vietnam | 2 Central African Republic |
| 3 Austria | 35 Kuwait | 3 Armenia | 35 Serbia | 3 Benin | 35 West Bank and Gaza | 3 Ethiopia |
| 4 Bahamas, The | 36 Latvia | 4 Azerbaijan | 36 South Africa | 4 Bolivia | 36 Zambia | 4 Madagascar |
| 5 Bahrain | 37 Liechtenstein | 5 Belarus | 37 St. Lucia | 5 Cabo Verde | 37 Zimbabwe | 5 Malawi |
| 6 Barbados | 38 Lithuania | 6 Bosnia and Herzegovina | 38 Thailand | 6 Cambodia | | 6 Mali |
| 7 Belgium | 39 Luxembourg | 7 Botswana | 39 Türkiye | 7 Cameroon | | 7 Rwanda |
| 8 Bermuda | 40 Malta | 8 Brazil | | 8 Congo, Rep. | | 8 Sierra Leone |
| 9 British Virgin Islands | 41 Mauritius | 9 Bulgaria | | 9 Côte d'Ivoire | | 9 Tajikistan |
| 10 Brunei Darussalam | 42 Monaco | 10 China | | 10 Egypt, Arab Rep. | | 10 Togo |
| 11 Canada | 43 Netherlands | 11 Colombia | | 11 El Salvador | | 11 Uganda |
| 12 Cayman Islands | 44 New Zealand | 12 Costa Rica | | 12 Eswatini | | |
| 13 Chile | 45 Norway | 13 Ecuador | | 13 Ghana | | |
| 14 Croatia | 46 Oman | 14 Fiji | | 14 India | | |
| 15 Curaçao | 47 Panama | 15 Georgia | | 15 Kenya | | |
| 16 Cyprus | 48 Poland | 16 Guatemala | | 16 Kyrgyz Republic | | |
| 17 Czechia | 49 Portugal | 17 Indonesia | | 17 Lesotho | | |
| 18 Denmark | 50 Qatar | 18 Iran, Islamic Rep. | | 18 Mauritania | | |
| 19 Estonia | 51 Romania | 19 Iraq | | 19 Moldova | | |
| 20 Faroe Islands | 52 Saudi Arabia | 20 Jamaica | | 20 Mongolia | | |
| 21 Finland | 53 Seychelles | 21 Jordan | | 21 Morocco | | |
| 22 France | 54 Singapore | 22 Kazakhstan | | 22 Myanmar | | |
| 23 Germany | 55 Slovak Republic | 23 Kosovo | | 23 Nepal | | |
| 24 Gibraltar | 56 Slovenia | 24 Lebanon | | 24 Nigeria | | |
| 25 Greece | 57 Spain | 25 Libya | | 25 Pakistan | | |
| 26 Greenland | 58 Sweden | 26 Malaysia | | 26 Philippines | | |
| 27 Hong Kong SAR, China | 59 Switzerland | 27 Maldives | | 27 Senegal | | |
| 28 Hungary | 60 Taiwan, China | 28 Mexico | | 28 Solomon Islands | | |
| 29 Iceland | 61 United Arab Emirates | 29 Montenegro | | 29 Sri Lanka | | |
| 30 Ireland | 62 United Kingdom | 30 Namibia | | 30 Tanzania | | |
| 31 Israel | 63 United States | 31 North Macedonia | | 31 Tunisia | | |
| 32 Italy | 64 Uruguay | 32 Paraguay | | 32 Ukraine | | |

*Note:* Economies are classified according to the World Bank Classification of Countries as of June 2020.

# Notes

1. The empirical evidence is consistent with the view that credit constraints hinder investments in innovative activities. Research has shown that greater financial development tends to ease financial constraints and allows more resources to flow toward promising entrepreneurs, accelerating technological innovation and economic growth. See, for example, Akcigit, Grigsby, and Nicholas (2017); Amore, Schneider, and Zaldokas (2013); Brown, Fazzari, and Petersen (2009); Brown, Martinsson, and Petersen (2012, 2013, 2017); Chava et al. (2013); Cornaggia et al. (2015); Fang, Tian, and Tice (2014); Hsu, Tian, and Xu (2014); Laeven, Levine, and Michalopoulos (2015); and Madsen and Ang (2016).

2. A relatively small but growing literature focuses on financing R&D with equity issues. See, for example, Aghion et al. (2012); Borisova and Brown (2013); Brown, Fazzari, and Petersen (2009); Brown and Floros (2012); Brown and Petersen (2011); Campello and Hackbarth (2012); Duval, Hong, and Timmer (2017); Gompers and Lerner (2001); Kortum and Lerner (2000); Sasidharan, Lukose, and Komera (2015); and Scellato (2007).

3. From the perspective of firms, equity financing is a potential source of external funding only when entrepreneurs are willing to undergo substantial dilution in terms of their equity ownership as well as cede control to equity investors, such as venture capitalists. Family ownership, for example, has been associated with a reluctance to accept external shareholders, regardless of economic or financial considerations. These firms would tend to raise capital through external debt rather than equity to preserve both ownership and control. See, for example, Berrone et al. (2010); Cruz, Gómez-Mejia, and Becerra (2010); Gómez-Mejía et al. (2007); Gómez-Mejía et al. (2011); Gonzalez et al. (2013); and Schmid (2013).

4. The literature finds a negative association between R&D and leverage across firms—see Hall and Lerner (2010) for a survey.

5. See, for example, Bernstein, Giroud, and Townsend (2016); Davila, Foster, and Gupta (2003); Engel and Keilbach (2007); Hirukawa and Ueda (2008); Kortum and Lerner (2000); Puri and Zarutskie (2012); Samila and Sorenson (2010, 2011); and Schnitzer and Watzinger (2022).

6. While the volume of financing when measured as a share of gross domestic product tends to be significantly larger in PE markets than in VC markets across EMDEs (figure 3.1), a smaller number of firms obtain PE financing than VC financing in these countries. In other words, PE markets tend to provide larger financing amounts to a smaller set of firms than VC markets in EMDEs.

7. The experience of HICs indicates that supporting equity market development is a costly endeavor, often with long lead times, and it requires a long-term commitment to ensure the effectiveness of public policies.

8. The ownership and governance of VC investors is an important source of heterogeneity within VC investments. For example, evidence from VC investments in the United States and Europe shows that corporate VC investors are particularly attracted to companies operating in industries with high-tech activities and weak intellectual property protection—such as internet and telecommunications services—and they tend to refrain from investing in biotechnology and pharmaceuticals, where intellectual property can be effectively protected (Bertoni, Colombo, and Quas 2015). Bank-affiliated VC investors in Europe are more likely to invest in older and larger companies and locally, where they can exploit their superior ability to gather soft information (Coval and Moskowitz 2001; Fritsch and Schilder 2008).

9. According to PitchBook, company verticals represent a specific investment area of focus that cannot be accurately depicted by a company industry group alone. Verticals commonly span across industries, such that companies tagged to a vertical may belong to a variety of different industries.

10. For example, there has been a substantial increase in capital available for more mature, late-stage start-ups more recently in the United States (Ewens and Farre-Mensa 2022).

11. See, for example, Da Rin, Hellmann, and Puri (2013) and the references therein, which are largely focused on HICs.

12. Hence, large firms would generally have more diversified, less volatile earnings and lower default risk than small and young firms—which are particularly susceptible to problems of financial distress and failure. Firm size can be considered an inverse proxy for bankruptcy probability. See, for example, Coleman, Cotei, and Farhat (2013) and Fama and French (2002).

13. The index is published by the IESE Business School and captures a wide range of factors underlying the development of the VC segment, including those related to the enabling environment for the VC industry as well as the availability of investment opportunities and capital.

14. If equity investments through private markets are made in situations where informational asymmetries are severe and remain so at the exit stage, then it may be difficult to exit through an IPO as most public investors are relatively uninformed. In this case, investor exit will be dominated by private deals rather than IPOs.

15. For example, Lerner and Nanda (2020) show that VC–backed firms represented more than half of the companies that went public between 1995 and 2018.

16. Consistently, the U.S. National Venture Capital Association (2020) estimates that IPOs have accounted for only 10 percent of exits for venture-backed start-ups in recent years, with the rest occurring mostly through acquisitions.

17. Equity investors in private markets might try to build a reputation for presenting good quality firms in public offerings. Therefore, IPO exits would tend to be drawn from the better performing firms. See, for example, Cochrane (2005), Cumming and MacIntosh (2003), Darby and Zucker (2002), Gompers (1995), and Gompers and Lerner (1999).

18. Public equity markets can also support private markets for equity financing along other dimensions. For example, Gompers et al. (2008) provide evidence that public equity markets can provide signals of investment opportunities to equity investors in private markets.

19. See, for example, Botelho, Fehder, and Hochberg (2021); Janeway, Nanda, and Rhodes-Kropf (2021); and Lerner and Nanda (2020) and the references therein.

20. Mason and Kwok (2010) highlight three main aspects of this lack of investment readiness. First, many entrepreneurs are unwilling to surrender ownership and control of their firms through equity investments. Second, many businesses that seek external finance are not considered "investible" by external investors because of deficiencies in their team structure, marketing strategy, financial accounts, intellectual property protection, and other business areas. Third, even if entrepreneurs are willing to consider equity and have investible projects, presentational failings mean that many firms are unable to pitch their ideas successfully to investors. See also Cirera et al. (2020) and references therein.

## References

Aghion, P., P. Askenazy, N. Berman, G. Cette, and L. Eymard. 2012. "Credit Constraints and the Cyclicality of R&D Investment: Evidence from France." *Journal of the European Economic Association* 10: 1001–24.

Akcigit, U., J. Grigsby, and T. Nicholas. 2017. "The Rise of American Ingenuity: Innovation and Inventors of the Golden Age." Working Paper 23047, National Bureau of Economic Research, Cambridge, MA.

Amore, M., C. Schneider, and A. Zaldokas. 2013. "Credit Supply and Corporate Innovation." *Journal of Financial Economics* 109: 835–55.

Bernstein, S., X. Giroud, and R. R. Townsend. 2016. "The Impact of Venture Capital Monitoring." *Journal of Finance* 71 (4): 1591–622.

Berrone, P., C. Cruz, L. Gómez-Mejía, and M. Larraza-Kintana. 2010. "Socioemotional Wealth and Corporate Responses to Institutional Pressures: Do Family-Controlled Firms Pollute Less?" *Administrative Science Quarterly* 55 (1): 82–113.

Bertoni, F., M. Colombo, and A. Quas. 2015. "The Patterns of Venture Capital Investment in Europe." *Small Business Economics* 45: 543–60.

Borisova, G., and J. R. Brown. 2013. "R&D Sensitivity to Asset Sale Proceeds: New Evidence on Financing Constraints and Intangible Investment." *Journal of Banking and Finance* 37 (1): 159–73.

Botelho, T., D. Fehder, and Y. Hochberg. 2021. "Innovation-Driven Entrepreneurship." NBER Working Paper 28990, National Bureau of Economic Research, Cambridge, MA.

Brown, J. R., S. M. Fazzari, and B. C. Petersen. 2009. "Financing Innovation and Growth: Cash Flow, External Equity, and the 1990s R&D Boom." *Journal of Finance* 64 (1): 151–85.

Brown, J. R., and I. V. Floros. 2012. "Access to Private Equity and Real Firm Activity: Evidence from PIPEs." *Journal of Corporate Finance* 18 (1): 151–65.

Brown, J. R., G. Martinsson, and B. C. Petersen. 2012. "Do Financing Constraints Matter for R&D?" *European Economic Review* 56 (8): 1512–29.

Brown, J. R., G. Martinsson, and B. C. Petersen. 2013. "Law, Stock Markets, and Innovation." *Journal of Finance* 68 (4): 1517–49.

Brown, J. R., G. Martinsson, and B. C. Petersen. 2017. "Stock Markets, Credit Markets, and Technology-Led Growth." *Journal of Financial Intermediation* 32: 45–59.

Brown, J. R., and B. C. Petersen. 2011. "Cash Holdings and R&D Smoothing." *Journal of Corporate Finance* 17 (3): 694–709.

Campello, M., and D. Hackbarth. 2012. "The Firm-Level Credit Multiplier." *Journal of Financial Intermediation* 21: 446–72.

Chava, S., A. Oettl, A. Subramanian, and K. Subramanian. 2013. "Banking Deregulation and Innovation." *Journal of Financial Economics* 109: 759–74.

Cirera, X., J. Frías, J. Hill, and Y. Li. 2020. *A Practitioner's Guide to Innovation Policy: Instruments to Build Firm Capabilities and Accelerate Technological Catch-Up in Developing Countries.* Washington, DC: World Bank.

Cochrane, J. 2005. "The Risk and Return of Venture Capital." *Journal of Financial Economics* 75: 3–52.

Coleman, S., C. Cotei, and J. Farhat. 2013. "A Resource-Based View of New Firm Survival: New Perspectives on the Role of Industry and Exit Route." *Journal of Development Entrepreneurship* 18 (1): 1350002.

Cornaggia, J., Y. Mao, X. Tian, and B. Wolfe. 2015. "Does Banking Competition Affect Innovation?" *Journal of Financial Economics* 115 (1): 189–209.

Coval, J., and T. Moskowitz. 2001. "The Geography of Investment: Informed Trading and Asset Prices." *Journal of Political Economy* 109: 811–41.

Cruz, C., L. Gómez-Mejia, and M. Becerra. 2010. "Perceptions of Benevolence and the Design of Agency Contracts: CEO-TMT Relationships in Family Firms." *Academy of Management Journal* 53 (1): 69–89.

Cumming, D. J., and J. G. Maclntosh. 2003. "A Cross-Country Comparison of Full and Partial Venture Capital Exits." *Journal of Banking and Finance* 27 (3): 511–48.

Da Rin, M., T. Hellmann, and M. Puri. 2013. "A Survey of Venture Capital Research." In *Handbook of the Economics of Finance*, vol. 2, edited by G. M. Constantinides, M. Harris, and R. M. Stulz, 573–648. Elsevier.

Darby, M., and L. Zucker. 2002. "Going Public When You Can in Biotechnology." NBER Working Paper 8954, National Bureau of Economic Research, Cambridge, MA.

Davila, A., G. Foster, and M. Gupta. 2003. "Venture Capital Financing and the Growth of Start-up Firms." *Journal of Business Ventures* 18 (6): 689–708.

Didier, T., and B. Cheuva. 2023. "Private Markets for Equity Financing in Developing Countries." Background paper for this volume. World Bank, Washington, DC.

Duval, R., G. Hong, and Y. Timmer. 2017. "Financial Frictions and the Great Productivity Slowdown." IMF Working Paper 17/129, International Monetary Fund, Washington, DC.

Engel, D., and M. Keilbach. 2007. "Firm Level Implications of Early-Stage Venture Capital Investments: An Empirical Investigation." *Journal of Empirical Finance* 14: 150–67.

Ewens, M., and J. Farre-Mensa. 2022. "Private or Public Equity? The Evolving Entrepreneurial Finance Landscape." *Annual Review of Financial Economics* 14: 271–93.

Fama, E., and K. R. French. 2002. "Testing Trade-off and Pecking Order Predictions about Dividends and Debt." *Review of Financial Studies* 15 (1): 1–33.

Fang, V., X. Tian, and S. Tice. 2014. "Does Stock Liquidity Enhance or Impede Firm Innovation?" *Journal of Finance* 69: 2085–2125.

Fritsch, M., and D. Schilder. 2008. "Does Venture Capital Investment Really Require Spatial Proximity? An Empirical Investigation." *Environment and Planning* 40: 2114–31.

Gómez-Mejía, L. R., C. Cruz, P. Berrone, and J. De Castro. 2011. "The Bind That Ties: Socioemotional Wealth Preservation in Family Firms." *Academy of Management Annals* 5 (1): 653–707.

Gómez-Mejía, L. R., K. Takacs-Haynes, M. Núñez-Nickel, K. J. L. Jacobson, and J. Moyano-Fuentes. 2007. "Socioemotional Wealth and Business Risks in Family-Controlled Firms: Evidence from Spanish Olive Oil Mills." *Administrative Science Quarterly* 52 (1): 106–37.

Gompers, P. A. 1995. "Optimal Investment, Monitoring, and the Staging of Venture Capital." *Journal of Finance* 50: 1461–89.

Gompers, P., A. Kovner, J. Lerner, and D. Scharfstein. 2008. "Venture Capital Investment Cycles: The Impact of Public Markets." *Journal of Financial Economics* 87 (1): 1–23.

Gompers, P., and J. Lerner. 1999. *The Venture Capital Cycle*. Cambridge, MA: MIT Press.

Gompers, P., and J. Lerner. 2001. "The Venture Capital Revolution." *Journal of Economic Perspectives* 15: 45–62.

González, M., A. Guzmán, C. Pombo, and M.-A. Trujillo. 2013. "Family Firms and Debt: Risk Aversion versus Risk of Losing Control." *Journal of Business Research* 66 (11): 2308–20.

Guery, L., A. Stevenot, G. T. Wood, and C. Brewster. 2017. "The Impact of Private Equity on Employment: The Consequences of Fund Country of Origin—New Evidence from France." *Industrial Relations: A Journal of Economy and Society* 56 (4): 723–50.

Hall, B. H. 2002. "The Financing of Research and Development." *Oxford Review of Economic Policy* 18 (1): 35–51.

Hall, B. H., and J. Lerner. 2010. "The Financing of R&D and Innovation." In *Handbook of the Economics of Innovation*, vol. 1, edited by B. H. Hall and N. Rosenberg, 609–40. Amsterdam: North-Holland.

Hellman, T., P. Schure, and D. H. Vo. 2021. "Angels and Venture Capitalists: Substitutes or Complements?" *Journal of Financial Economics* 141: 454–78.

Hirukawa, M., and M. Ueda. 2008. "Venture Capital and Industrial Innovation." CEPR Discussion Paper 7089, Center for Economic and Policy Research, Washington, DC.

Hsu, P. H., X. Tian, and Y. Xu. 2014. "Financial Development and Innovation: Cross-Country Evidence." *Journal of Financial Economics* 112: 116–35.

Janeway, W. H., R. Nanda, and M. Rhodes-Kropf. 2021. "Venture Capital Booms and Startup Financing." *Annual Review of Financial Economics* 13: 111–27.

Kortum, S., and J. Lerner. 2000. "Assessing the Contribution of Venture Capital to Innovation." *RAND Journal of Economics* 31 (4): 674–92.

Laeven, L., R. Levine, and S. Michalopoulos. 2015. "Financial Innovation and Endogenous Growth." *Journal of Financial Intermediation* 24 (1): 1–24.

Lerner, J. 2008. *Boulevard of Broken Dreams: Why Public Efforts to Boost Entrepreneurship and Venture Capital Have Failed.* Princeton, NJ: Princeton University Press.

Lerner, J. 2013. "The Boulevard of Broken Dreams: Innovation Policy and Entrepreneurship." *Innovation Policy and the Economy* 13 (1): 61–82.

Lerner, J., J. Ledbetter, A. Speen, A. Leamon, and C. Allen. 2016. "Private Equity in Emerging Markets: Yesterday, Today, and Tomorrow." *Journal of Private Equity* 19 (3): 8–20.

Lerner, J., and R. Nanda. 2020. "Venture Capital's Role in Financing Innovation: What We Know and How Much We Still Need to Learn." *Journal of Economic Perspectives* 34 (3): 237–61.

Madsen, J. B., and J. B. Ang. 2016. "Finance-Led Growth in the OECD Since the Nineteenth Century: How Does Financial Development Transmit to Growth?" *Review of Economics and Statistics* 98 (3): 552–72.

Mason, C., and J. Kwok. 2010. "Investment Readiness Programmes and Access to Finance: A Critical Review of Design Issues." *Local Economy* 25 (4): 269–92.

National Venture Capital Association. 2020. "NVCA 2020 Yearbook." National Venture Capital Association, Washington, DC (accessed April 1, 2020), https://nvca.org/wp-content/uploads/2020/04/NVCA-2020-Yearbook.pdf.

PitchBook. 2023. "Private Equity vs. Venture Capital: What's the Difference?" *PitchBook Blog*, February 4, 2023. https://pitchbook.com/blog/private-equity-vs-venture-capital-whats-the-difference.

Puri, M., and R. Zarutskie. 2012. "On the Life Cycle Dynamics of Venture-Capital- and Non-Venture-Capital-Financed Firms." *Journal of Finance* 67 (6): 2247–93.

Samila, S., and O. Sorenson. 2010. "Venture Capital as a Catalyst to Innovation." *Research Policy* 39: 1348–60.

Samila, S., and O. Sorenson. 2011. "Venture Capital, Entrepreneurship, and Economic Growth." *Review of Economics and Statistics* 93 (1): 338–49.

Sasidharan, S., P. J. J. Lukose, and S. Komera. 2015. "Financing Constraints and Investments in R&D: Evidence from Indian Manufacturing Firms." *Quarterly Review of Economics and Finance* 55: 28–39.

Scellato, G. 2007. "Patents, Firm Size and Financial Constraints: An Empirical Analysis for a Panel of Italian Manufacturing Firms." *Cambridge Journal of Economics* 31 (1): 55–76.

Schmid, T. 2013. "Control Considerations, Creditor Monitoring, and the Capital Structure of Family Firms." *Journal of Banking and Finance* 37: 257–72.

Schnitzer, M., and M. Watzinger. 2022. "Measuring the Spillovers of Venture Capital." *Review of Economics and Statistics* 104 (2): 276–92.

# 4. Within-Firm Dynamics: Financing Firms' Growth

**Key Messages**

- **This chapter quantifies the direct links among firm financing, its composition (debt versus equity financing), the composition of firms' subsequent investments, and firms' overall performance.** It thus sheds light on the mechanisms through which financial markets support firms' investments in productive capabilities and growth.

- **Firms experience a boost in growth and productive capabilities by raising funds in capital markets.** Firms that issue in capital markets use the funds raised to grow by enhancing their productive capabilities, increasing their tangible and intangible capital, and the number of employees. Growth accelerates as firms raise financing in capital markets. Moreover, firms that experience exogenous changes in growth opportunities are more likely to issue securities in capital markets, suggesting that firms use capital markets to realize growth opportunities by expanding their productive capabilities.

- **Firms that are ex ante more likely to be financially constrained tend to experience a larger boost in growth around capital market financing,** especially smaller firms and firms with high levels of research and development (R&D). These results suggest that capital markets can allow financially constrained firms to relax their funding restrictions and grow.

- **The composition of financing sources is quantitatively important for firm performance.** For instance, equity but not bond issuance is associated with more rapid expansions of the productive capabilities of high R&D firms, especially in terms of intangible assets. This suggests that equity may be a more effective way of financing the growth of innovative firms. The findings are consistent with evidence from industry-level studies that show that more developed equity (but not debt) markets are important for innovation inputs. The implication is that limited access to equity financing impacts and can distort investment decisions, thereby affecting firm productivity and growth.

## Introduction

Financial constraints have a significant impact on firms' investments in productive capabilities and growth—the *within* margin discussed in the conceptual framework presented in chapter 1. Chapters 2 and 3 provided a quantitative assessment of the extent of financial constraints on firms in middle-income countries (MICs). The rest of this volume takes this evidence a step further and shows that these constraints reflect inefficiencies in the allocation of capital, especially for smaller firms in MICs,

---

This chapter is based on Didier et al. (2021), a background paper for this volume.

with sizable impacts on aggregate outcomes. The volume provides novel evidence supporting this hypothesis along two margins: improved firm performance (the *within* margin) and improved allocation of resources across firms (the *between* margin). This chapter focuses on the former.

Although the literature has shown positive links between capital market development and national growth rates, it does not necessarily imply that firms use the funds raised in these markets to increase their productive capabilities—human capital, physical capital, and intangible capital—and grow.[1] Existing research tends to be silent on the use of capital markets in particular, and external financing sources more broadly, to fund corporate investments in productive capabilities and growth.[2] There is limited evidence on the role of public equity and debt markets in fostering the productivity and growth of firms, especially in emerging market and developing economies (EMDEs), and the few studies that have done so use aggregate country- or industry-level data.

This chapter sheds light on these issues by presenting new empirical evidence of how firms in MICs and high-income countries (HICs) that raise capital through various sources use the proceeds to boost their productive capabilities. The analysis also sheds light on whether the additional financing from new capital raising allows financially constrained firms to improve their performance. To the extent that financing constraints prevented firms from exploiting growth opportunities, relaxing these constraints through new capital raising issuances of debt or equity would likely be associated with larger increases in investments than if those firms faced less restrictive financing constraints prior to issuing securities. Overall, the analysis characterizes the direct links among firm financing, its composition (debt versus equity financing), the composition of firms' subsequent investments, and firms' overall performance. It thus sheds light on the mechanisms through which financial markets support firms' investments in productive capabilities and growth. Box 4.1 describes the data and methodology behind the analysis in this chapter.

---

**BOX 4.1**

### Data and Methodology

The findings in this chapter are drawn from: (1) more than 150,000 capital market issuances of debt and (public) equity in domestic and international markets during 1991–2016, and (2) a comprehensive sample of more than 62,000 publicly listed firms in 65 countries (see annex 4A for the sample of countries). The data include firms with capital raising issuances as well as firms that did not raise capital in these markets during the sample period.

A difference-in-difference empirical strategy is adopted, comparing firms that raised new financing to otherwise similar firms that did not do so during the same phase of their life cycles.[a] The results provide econometric estimates of the changes in the effects of firms' capital raising activity on firm performance (growth in total assets and total sales) and changes in investment

*(Box continues on the following page.)*

Unleashing Productivity through Firm Finance

composition measured by the potential uses of the capital raised—namely, the number of employees, tangible fixed assets, intangible assets, expenditures on research and development (R&D), inventories, and cash holdings. Importantly, the analysis explores whether these direct links between finance and growth vary across firms' life cycles (measured by firm size and age). It also explores whether the sources of firm financing matter for firms' growth in productive capabilities, building on the hypothesis that equity finance might be more effective at funding innovative, riskier firms. In addition, the analysis investigates whether the returns to finance are greater for firms that are more likely to be financially constrained, such as small, young, high R&D firms. Lastly, the analysis examines whether a country's financial architecture (bank-based versus market-based financial systems) shapes which types of firms obtain financing, thereby affecting the composition of firms in a given country.

a. Additional controls in the estimations include time variant, firm-level characteristics and country-year, and firm fixed effects.

## Firm Financing and Increases in Productive Capabilities

Firms experience a boost in sales and total assets and an increase in productive capabilities—tangible assets (proxied by property, plant, and equipment), intangible assets, and employment—by raising funds in capital markets. Compared to nonissuers, firms that issue securities, referred to as "issuers," grow faster before, during, and after the capital raising issuance of securities, with the growth differential significantly widening in the aftermath of the issuance. The estimates indicate significant cumulative growth differentials in sales, assets, and productive capabilities for issuers relative to nonissuers around a five-year issuance window. For example, the cumulative growth differential in terms of the number of employees is estimated to be about 18 percentage points between issuing and nonissuing firms. Issuing firms also increased their capital expenditures: property, plant, and equipment increased by 32 percentage points more than for nonissuing firms, and intangible assets increased by 39 percentage points more.

The results on increases in tangible and intangible assets as well as employment strongly suggest that a motive behind equity and bond issuances is to raise capital to finance investment. That is, the funds raised are not simply used to rebalance firms' financial accounts—research has argued that firms could raise capital to pay off liabilities, replace more expensive financing with cheaper funding, minimize taxes, or change the duration of debt.[3] It is important that an increase in total assets would not necessarily translate into a material increase in productive capabilities, as firms can also use the funds to accumulate cash and make financial investments, acting as financial intermediaries.[4]

The increase in investments in productive capabilities and growth around capital market financing is larger for firms issuing equity than for firms issuing bonds (figure 4.1). [5,6] For example, the growth differential in sales over a five-year window around issuances between issuing firms and nonissuing firms is on average 18 percentage points for equity issuers, whereas this growth acceleration is about 8 percentage points for bond issuers. A similar differential of about 9 percentage points in growth between equity and bond issuers is estimated for total assets. Equity issuers grow faster than bond issuers even though equity issuances tend to be smaller—the median equity issue was US$20.55 million per issuance, whereas the median bond was US$77.91 million.

**FIGURE 4.1   Cumulative Growth Differential for Issuing Firms Relative to Nonissuing Firms around Capital Raising Activity**

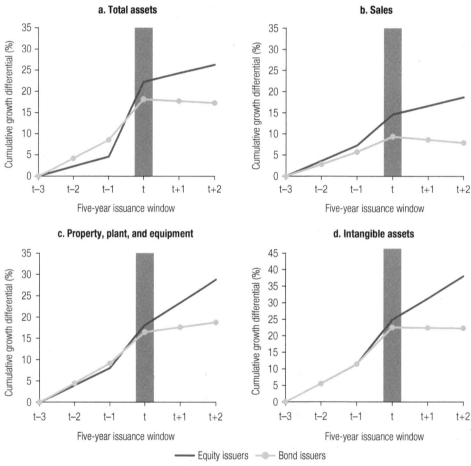

*Source:* Calculations based on Didier et al. 2021.

*Note:* This figure shows the estimated cumulative growth differential between issuers and nonissuers around a five-year issuance window. It shows the growth differentials for total assets; sales; property, plant, and equipment; and intangible assets. The figure considers two types of issuing firms: equity issuers and bond issuers. For each definition, the figure shows the cumulative growth differential around the issuance years compared to the growth rate of all the firms in the sample during their nonissuance years. Year t refers to the year of issuance. Growth rates for both issuers and nonissuers are normalized to 0 in year t–3. The years t–2 and t–1 (t+2 and t+1) refer to the pre-issuance (post-issuance) period.

Moreover, equity financing is in practice associated with greater investments in intangible assets than debt financing. The increase in intangible assets around new financing is marked when contrasting equity and bond issuers: intangible assets grow 16 percentage points faster for equity issuers than bond issuers, whereas tangible fixed assets expand 10 percentage points faster. These results reinforce the findings in chapter 3, suggesting that equity contracts are used to finance innovative activities, which typically entail riskier investments in intangible assets with limited collateral value.

## Larger Effects for ex ante Financially Constrained Firms

The relationship between firms' investments in productive capabilities and growth, and capital raising activity is expected to be stronger among firms with tighter financing constraints, for which the marginal returns to increasing human, tangible, and intangible capital are likely to be greater. To the extent that firms have limited access to other sources of financing, the growth differential between issuing and nonissuing firms would likely be larger for financially constrained firms because they have fewer alternatives for relieving such constraints. Similarly, to the extent that financing constraints prevented firms from exploiting growth opportunities, relaxing these constraints through the issuances of stocks or bonds would likely be associated with larger increases in productive capabilities than if those firms faced less restrictive financing constraints before issuing securities.

The results confirm this hypothesis: firms that are ex ante more likely to be financially constrained—for example, small firms—tend to experience a larger boost in growth and productive capabilities around capital market financing (figure 4.2).[7] For example, in the year of issuance, the growth rate of total assets for firms at the bottom of the size distribution (the smallest firms in the sample) is on average 37 percentage points faster that for similarly sized nonissuing firms. In contrast, this differential for firms at the top of the size distribution (the largest firms in the sample) is about 7 percentage points, which is still economically significant as it is 56 percent larger than the average growth of gross domestic product (4.4 percent) across countries in the sample. Qualitatively similar patterns are estimated for firm growth in sales, number of employees, research and development (R&D) expenditures, tangible fixed assets, and intangible assets.

Similar patterns are observed among high R&D firms, which arguably face more stringent financing constraints because of their greater investments in intangible assets. When classified according to the degree of R&D intensity, issuing firms in the top 10 percent of the distribution (high R&D firms) grow almost 24 percentage points faster in terms of assets than those in the bottom 10 percent. These results hold not only when comparing firms at the extremes of the distribution, but also when observing the entire distribution. That is, the growth differential between issuers and nonissuers

## FIGURE 4.2    Cumulative Growth Differential across Issuing Firms

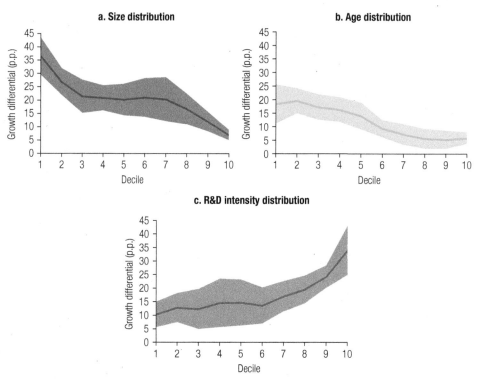

**a. Size distribution**

**b. Age distribution**

**c. R&D intensity distribution**

*Source:* Calculations based on Didier et al. 2021.

*Note:* This figure shows the estimated differential in the annual growth rate of total assets between issuers and nonissuers at the year of issuance for each decile of the distributions of firm size (panel a), firm age (panel b), and R&D intensity (panel c). The statistics were obtained from estimation of quantile regressions for each decile of the distribution. The shaded area shows the confidence interval around the estimates at the 95% statistical confidence level. Firm size is measured as the log of total assets; R&D intensity is the log of R&D in total investment. Firms are assigned to each decile based on their median size, age, and R&D intensity over the sample period. p.p. = percentage points; R&D = research and development.

monotonically declines along the deciles of the firm size and age distributions, and it monotonically increases along the R&D intensity distribution.

Furthermore, the results from the analysis of the direct links among firm financing, R&D, and firm growth show that equity (but not bond issuances) is associated with rapid post-issuance expansions of the productive capabilities of high R&D firms, especially in intangible assets.[8] This finding corroborates that equity issuances are a more effective way of financing the growth of innovative firms than debt issuances. For example, in the year of raising capital through equity, the growth rate of employment is 1.9 percentage points faster for high R&D firms than for other issuing firms. Importantly, the estimations show that the growth of intangible assets is 2.8 percentage points higher for high R&D issuers than for the other issuers in the year of an equity issuance— equivalent to approximately 28 percent of the average growth in intangibles for firms in the sample—and this differential increases to 4.2 percentage points during the

Unleashing Productivity through Firm Finance

post-issuance years. Meanwhile, there is no difference during the pre-issuance years. The estimates also show no quantitatively relevant growth differential for investments in tangible fixed assets nor around bond issuances.

These estimations are consistent with evidence from industry-level studies that show that more developed equity (but not debt) markets are important for innovation inputs (Brown, Martinsson, and Petersen 2013) and innovation outputs as measured by patents (Hsu, Tian, and Xu 2014), and they support faster growth of high-tech industries (Brown, Martinsson, and Petersen 2017). These effects work mostly through higher productivity growth rather than fixed capital accumulation. For example, for a sample of firms across 32 countries, Brown, Martinsson, and Petersen (2013) find that better access to equity financing leads to substantially higher long-run rates of R&D investment, particularly in small, listed firms, but it is unimportant for fixed capital investment. In contrast, debt market development has a modest impact on fixed investment but no impact on R&D.

Although the estimations do not capture the effects across private firms (because of significant data constraints), these results could be interpreted as lower bound estimates of the relationship between financing and growth for private firms. That is, even within the universe of publicly listed firms, for which the financing constraint problems are significantly less marked, as discussed in chapter 2, there is economically and statistically significant heterogeneity based on firm size, age, and the degree of innovation. Nonetheless, this remains an open empirical question as, among other things, there are differences in the types and terms of financing to which public and private firms have access.

## Financial Architecture May Play a Role

There is a strong relationship between the structure of a country's financial system and the composition of listed firms. Regression estimates indicate that greater capital market development relative to bank development is associated with larger shares of smaller, younger, and more R&D-intensive firms among publicly listed firms (figure 4.3). For example, a firm at the 25th percentile of the size distribution has on average US$11.73 million in assets in countries with market-based financial systems, whereas a firm at the same percentile in countries with bank-based systems has on average US$65.43 million. Similarly, for countries with market-based financial systems, the distribution of firm R&D expenditures falls to the right of the distribution for countries with bank-based financial systems. For instance, a firm at the 75th percentile of the R&D distribution invests on average US$15.78 million in R&D in countries with market-based financial systems, whereas a firm at the same percentile of the distribution invests on average US$9.89 million in countries with bank-based financial systems. These results suggest that a country's financial architecture may shape which types of firms obtain financing, thereby affecting the composition of firms.

## FIGURE 4.3 Distributions of Listed Firms across Countries

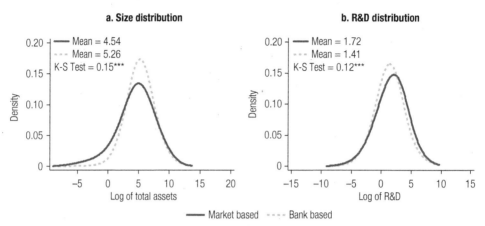

*Source:* Didier et al. 2021.

*Note:* This figure shows the estimated kernel distributions of the log of firm size and R&D for countries with market-based (solid line) and bank-based (dashed line) financial systems. Countries are classified as market based (bank based) if their average ratio of capital market to bank development during 1991–2016 was in the top (bottom) 25th percentile of the distribution across countries. The figure also shows the Kolmogorov-Smirnov (K-S) tests of equality of distributions. R&D = research and development.

\*\*\* denotes statistical significance at 1 percent.

## Changes in Growth Opportunities

A concern about characterizing within-firm growth-finance patterns using a difference-in-difference approach is that although the results are consistent with issuing firms observing growth opportunities and using the capital raised to realize these opportunities, growth opportunities at the firm level are not observable. An examination of how firms in the mining industry around the world respond to observable changes in growth opportunities sheds light on this issue. Shocks to the value of production in the mining sector can be proxied by changes in the prices of mining commodities. The underlying notion is that changes in mining prices shape the growth opportunities for firms in the industry.

The analysis shows that firms that experience exogenous positive changes in growth opportunities are more likely to issue securities in capital markets. Mining firms that experience higher commodity prices are more likely to issue equity and bonds, compared to firms in other industries. The marginal effects of the estimations show that, for example, when the mining price index (measured as the weighted average of 18 mining commodity prices) increases from 50 to 100, the probability of issuance for mining firms jumps from 11 to 21 percent. Aside from any effect that global financial conditions might have on the probability of issuance, these results suggest that higher output prices induce firms to issue more equity and bonds.

## Conclusions

Based on the conceptual framework outlined in chapter 1, this chapter explored the within margin (which focuses on performance within the firm) by analyzing the direct links among firm financing, its composition (debt versus equity financing), the composition of firms' subsequent investments, and firms' overall performance. It thus shed light on the mechanisms through which financial markets support firms' investments in productive capabilities and growth.

Although the evidence presented in this chapter does not reject theories that predict that firms issue securities to reap the benefits of developed capital markets and rebalance their capital structure, it establishes that there is a strong, positive direct relationship between capital market financing and firm growth across a wide array of countries, with implications for long-run economic performance. Moreover, the chapter provided evidence that financial constraints have a significant impact on firm growth. The empirical results indicate that capital market financing allows firms, especially small firms, to relax their financial constraints and realize expected growth opportunities by expanding their productive capabilities. This indicates that firms are not using the new funds just to change their capital structure or increase financial investments. To the extent that firms with access to capital markets, such as publicly listed firms, are less financially constrained than private firms, even larger effects of relaxing financial constraints on growth would be expected for private firms.

The analysis also suggests that the composition of financing sources is quantitatively important for firm performance. That is, debt and equity markets play important but distinct roles in supporting firms' investments in productive capabilities and growth. The evidence indicates that equity financing is indeed a more effective way of funding the productive growth of small and innovative firms. Equity, not debt, is particularly important for expansion of the productive capabilities of high R&D firms, especially in terms of intangible assets. The implication of this result is that limited access to equity financing affects and may distort investment decisions, with an impact on firm productivity and growth. Indeed, this direct channel of financing R&D activity with equity could explain the estimated long-lasting impact of capital market liberalizations on countries' growth rates to the extent that the opening process leads to a permanent increase in the availability of external equity finance.[9]

The findings in this chapter thus highlight the importance of supporting equity market development for EMDEs. The results suggest that constraints in access to equity financing can have an impact on aggregate growth and productivity through the within margin. Specifically, the underdevelopment of equity markets could hinder investments in intangibles, limiting the undertaking of innovative activities. Moreover, small and innovative firms would likely be more severely affected than large firms.[10] Smaller and more innovative firms in MICs not only have more limited access to equity financing (partly due to the small size of private markets), but also tend to have less debt financing, compared with firms in HICs, as shown in chapters 2 and 3.

## Annex 4A Sample of Economies with Issuing and Nonissuing Firms in Debt and Equity Markets

| | | | |
|---|---|---|---|
| 1 Argentina | | 34 Mexico | |
| 2 Australia | | 35 Morocco | |
| 3 Austria | | 36 Netherlands | |
| 4 Belgium | | 37 New Zealand | |
| 5 Brazil | | 38 Nigeria | |
| 6 Bulgaria | | 39 Norway | |
| 7 Canada | | 40 Oman | |
| 8 Chile | | 41 Pakistan | |
| 9 China | | 42 Peru | |
| 10 Colombia | | 43 Philippines | |
| 11 Croatia | | 44 Poland | |
| 12 Denmark | | 45 Portugal | |
| 13 Egypt, Arab Rep. | | 46 Qatar | |
| 14 Finland | | 47 Romania | |
| 15 France | | 48 Russian Federation | |
| 16 Germany | | 49 Saudi Arabia | |
| 17 Greece | | 50 Singapore | |
| 18 Hong Kong SAR, China | | 51 South Africa | |
| 19 Hungary | | 52 Spain | |
| 20 India | | 53 Sri Lanka | |
| 21 Indonesia | | 54 Sweden | |
| 22 Ireland | | 55 Switzerland | |
| 23 Israel | | 56 Taiwan, China | |
| 24 Italy | | 57 Thailand | |
| 25 Japan | | 58 Tunisia | |
| 26 Jordan | | 59 Türkiye | |
| 27 Kazakhstan | | 60 Ukraine | |
| 28 Kenya | | 61 United Arab Emirates | |
| 29 Korea, Rep. | | 62 United Kingdom | |
| 30 Kuwait | | 63 United States | |
| 31 Lithuania | | 64 Venezuela, RB | |
| 32 Luxembourg | | 65 Vietnam | |
| 33 Malaysia | | | |

*Source:* Didier et al. 2021.

# Notes

1. Indeed, several researchers find that firms use the newly raised funds to alter their liabilities, including changing debt-to-equity ratios, replacing more expensive financing with cheaper funding, minimizing taxes, or changing their debt maturity (Alden 2014; Bass and Smith 2018; De Angelo, De Angelo, and Stulz 2010; Graham and Harvey 2001; Graham and Leary 2011; Hertzel and Li 2010; Makan and Demos 2012; Pagano, Panetta, and Zingales 1998; Shin and Zhao 2013). Focusing on firm assets, other work shows that firms use the funds raised through securities issuances to accumulate cash or other financial assets (Baker and Wurgler 2002; Bruno and Shin 2017; Calomiris et al. 2019; Calomiris, Larrain, and Schmukler 2021; McLean 2011; McLean and Zhao 2018).

2. Kim and Weisbach (2008) explore public equity offerings, and Rahaman (2011) explores the effects of capital structure on firm growth for a sample of about 5,200 public and private firms in the United Kingdom and Ireland.

3. See, for example, Alden (2014); Bass and Smith (2018); Fan (2019); Makan and Demos (2012); and Pagano, Panetta, and Zingales (1998).

4. See, for example, Baker and Wurgler (2002); Bruno and Shin (2017); De Angelo, De Angelo, and Stulz (2010); McLean (2011); and McLean and Zhao (2018).

5. These results are related to a strand of the literature that argues that high-growth and riskier firms are more likely to raise capital through equity than through debt. See Barclay, Marx, and Smith (2003); Billett, King, and Mauer (2007); Bolton and Freixas (2000); Gatchev, Spindt, and Tarhan (2009); Hosono (2003); Hovakimian, Hovakimian, and Tehranian (2004); Jensen and Meckling (1976); Johnson (2003); Myers (1977); and Rajan and Zingales (1995).

6. These estimations are robust to the exclusion of capital raising activity associated with mergers and acquisitions.

7. An extensive literature argues that smaller, younger, and more innovative firms tend to be more informationally opaque and have fewer tangible assets to offer as collateral, which create higher barriers to such firms raising external finance. See, for example, Beck et al. (2008); Beck and Demirgüç-Kunt (2006); Beck, Demirgüç-Kunt, and Maksimovic (2005); Carpenter and Petersen (2002); Carreira and Silva (2010); and Oliveira and Fortunato (2006). Similar reasoning also applies for publicly listed firms. Although these firms are subject to financial reporting and disclosure, more information is generated and analyzed for larger than for smaller firms. See, for example, Atiase (1985); Bhushan (1989); Chang, Dasgupta, and Hilary (2006); and Collins, Kothari, and Rayburn (1987).

8. A few studies examine the role of equity markets as a funding source for R&D investments across firms. For instance, Brown, Fazzari, and Petersen (2009) provide evidence that US firms, especially young firms, finance R&D with external equity. Similarly, Brown, Martinsson, and Petersen (2013) argue that external equity financing plays a major role in financing R&D, especially for small firms compared to large firms, in a sample of approximately 5,300 firms across 32 countries. More closely related to the reported results, Brown and Floros (2012) provide evidence of a direct connection between external equity financing through private placements and innovative activity as proxied by R&D expenditures at the firm level for a sample of US firms. For a sample of US listed firms, Hoberg and Maksimovic (2015) find that high-growth firms that desire external equity are among the most financially constrained firms. Following a negative shock, these equity constrained firms tend to respond by severely curtailing their R&D and capital expenditures.

9. See, for example, Bekaert, Harvey, and Lundblad (2005, 2011).

10. Small firms in countries like the United States contribute a large share of total R&D, and there is evidence that their R&D is more productive than the R&D of larger firms.

# References

Alden, W. 2014. "First Data to Raise $3.5 Billion to Reduce Debt." *The New York Times*, June 19.

Atiase, R. W. 1985. "Predisclosure Information, Firm Capitalization, and Security Price Behavior around Earnings Announcements." *Journal of Accounting Research* 23 (1): 21–36.

Baker, M., and J. Wurgler. 2002. "Market Timing and Capital Structure." *Journal of Finance* 57 (1): 1–32.

Barclay, M. J., L. M. Marx, and C. W. Smith. 2003. "The Joint Determination of Leverage and Maturity." *Journal of Corporate Finance* 9: 149–67.

Bass, D., and M. Smith. 2018. "Dell Has 49 Billion Reasons to Consider Going Public Again." Bloomberg, January 26.

Beck, T., and A. Demirgüç-Kunt. 2006. "Small and Medium-Size Enterprises: Access to Finance as a Growth Constraint." *Journal of Banking and Finance* 30 (11): 2931–43.

Beck, T., A. Demirgüç-Kunt, L. Laeven, and R. Levine. 2008. "Finance, Firm Size, and Growth." *Journal of Money, Credit and Banking* 40 (7): 1379–1405.

Beck, T., A. Demirgüç-Kunt, and V. Maksimovic. 2005. "Financial and Legal Constraints to Firm Growth: Does Size Matter?" *Journal of Finance* 60: 137–77.

Bekaert, G., C. Harvey, and C. Lundblad. 2005. "Does Financial Liberalization Spur Economic Growth?" *Journal of Financial Economics* 77 (1): 3–55.

Bekaert, G., C. Harvey, and C. Lundblad. 2011. "Financial Openness and Productivity." *World Development* 39 (1): 1–19.

Bhushan, R. 1989. "Firm Characteristics and Analyst Following." *Journal of Accounting and Economics* 11: 255–74.

Billett, M. T., T.-H. D. King, and D. C. Mauer. 2007. "Growth Opportunities and the Choice of Leverage, Debt Maturity, and Covenants." *Journal of Finance* 62 (2): 697–730.

Bolton, P., and X. Freixas. 2000. "Equity, Bonds, and Bank Debt: Capital Structure and Financial Market Equilibrium under Asymmetric Information." *Journal of Political Economy* 108 (2): 324–51.

Brown, J. R., S. M. Fazzari, and B. C. Petersen. 2009. "Financing Innovation and Growth: Cash Flow, External Equity, and the 1990s R&D Boom." *Journal of Finance* 64 (1): 151–85.

Brown, J. R., and I. V. Floros. 2012. "Access to Private Equity and Real Firm Activity: Evidence from PIPEs." *Journal of Corporate Finance* 18: 151–65.

Brown, J. R., G. Martinsson, and B. C. Petersen. 2013. "Law, Stock Markets, and Innovation." *Journal of Finance* 68 (4): 1517–49.

Brown, J. R., G. Martinsson, and B. C. Petersen. 2017. "Stock Markets, Credit Markets, and Technology-Led Growth." *Journal of Financial Intermediation* 32: 45–59.

Bruno, V., and H. Shin. 2017. "Global Dollar Credit and Carry Trades: A Firm-Level Analysis." *Review of Financial Studies* 30 (3): 703–49.

Calomiris, C., M. Larrain, and S. Schmukler. 2021. "Capital Inflows, Equity Issuance Activity, and Corporate Investment." *Journal of Financial Intermediation* 46: 100845.

Calomiris, C., M. Larrain, S. Schmukler, and T. Williams. 2019. "Search for Yield in Large International Corporate Bonds: Investor Behavior and Firm Responses." NBER Working Paper 25979, National Bureau of Economic Research, Cambridge, MA.

Carpenter, R. E., and B. C. Petersen. 2002. "Is the Growth of Small Firms Constrained by Internal Finance?" *Review of Economics and Statistics* 84 (2): 298–309.

Carreira, C., and F. Silva. 2010. "No Deep Pockets: Some Stylized Empirical Results on Firms' Financial Constraints." *Journal of Economic Surveys* 24 (4): 731–53.

Chang, X., S. Dasgupta, and G. Hilary. 2006. "Analyst Coverage and Financing Decisions." *Journal of Finance* 61 (6): 3009–48.

Collins, D. W., S. P. Kothari, and J. D. Rayburn. 1987. "Firm Size and the Information Content of Prices with Respect to Earnings." *Journal of Accounting and Economics* 9 (2): 111–38.

De Angelo, H., L. De Angelo, and R. Stulz. 2010. "Seasoned Equity Offerings, Market Timing, and the Corporate Lifecycle." *Journal of Financial Economics* 95 (1): 275–95.

Didier, T., R. Levine, R. Llovet Montanes, and S. L. Schmukler. 2021. "Capital Market Financing and Firm Growth." *Journal of International Money and Finance* 118: 102459.

Fan, P. 2019. "Debt Retirement at IPO and Firm Growth." *Journal of Economics and Business* 101: 1–16.

Gatchev, V. A., P. A. Spindt, and V. Tarhan. 2009. "How Do Firms Finance Their Investments? The Relative Importance of Equity Issuance and Debt Contracting Costs." *Journal of Corporate Finance* 15: 179–95.

Graham, J. R., and C. R. Harvey. 2001. "The Theory and Practice of Corporate Finance: Evidence from the Field." *Journal of Financial Economics* 60: 187–243.

Graham, J. R., and M. T. Leary. 2011. "A Review of Empirical Capital Structure Research and Directions for the Future." *Annual Review of Financial Economics* 3 (1): 309–45.

Hertzel, M., and Z. Li. 2010. "Behavioral and Rational Explanations of Stock Price Performance around SEOs: Evidence from a Decomposition of Market-to-Book Ratios." *Journal of Financial and Quantitative Analysis* 45 (4): 935–58.

Hoberg, G., and V. Maksimovic. 2015. "Redefining Financial Constraints: A Text-Based Analysis." *Review of Financial Studies* 28 (5): 1312–52.

Hosono, K. 2003. "Growth Opportunities, Collateral and Debt Structure: The Case of the Japanese Machine Manufacturing Firms." *Japan and the World Economy* 15: 275–97.

Hovakimian, A., G. Hovakimian, and H. Tehranian. 2004. "Determinants of Target Capital Structure: The Case of Dual Debt and Equity Issues." *Journal of Financial Economics* 71: 517–40.

Hsu, P.-H., X. Tian, and Y. Xu. 2014. "Financial Development and Innovation: Cross-Country Evidence." *Journal of Financial Economics* 112: 116–35.

Jensen, M. C., and W. H. Meckling. 1976. "Theory of the Firm: Managerial Behavior, Agency Costs, and Ownership Structure." *Journal of Financial Economics* 3 (4): 305–60.

Johnson, S. A. 2003. "Debt Maturity and the Effects of Growth Opportunities and Liquidity Risk on Leverage." *Review of Financial Studies* 16 (1): 209–36.

Kim, W., and M. S. Weisbach. 2008. "Motivations for Public Equity Offers: An International Perspective." *Journal of Financial Economics* 87: 281–307.

Makan, A., and T. Demos. 2012. "Apollo Unit Plans $1bn IPO to Reduce Debt." *Financial Times*, June 8.

McLean, R. D. 2011. "Share Issuance and Cash Savings." *Journal of Financial Economics* 99: 693–715.

McLean, R. D., and M. Zhao. 2018. "Cash Savings and Capital Markets." *Journal of Empirical Finance* 47: 49–64.

Myers, S. C. 1977. "Determinants of Corporate Borrowing." *Journal of Financial Economics* 5 (2): 147–75.

Oliveira, B., and A. Fortunato. 2006. "Firm Growth and Liquidity Constraints: A Dynamic Analysis." *Small Business Economics* 27 (2–3): 139–56.

Pagano, M., F. Panetta, and L. Zingales. 1998. "Why Do Companies Go Public? An Empirical Analysis." *Journal of Finance* 53 (1): 27–64.

Rahaman, M. M. 2011. "Access to Financing and Firm Growth." *Journal of Banking and Finance* 35 (3): 709–23.

Rajan, R. G., and L. Zingales. 1995. "What Do We Know about Capital Structure? Some Evidence from International Data." *Journal of Finance* 50 (5): 1421–60.

Shin, H., and L. Zhao. 2013. "Firms as Surrogate Intermediaries: Evidence from Emerging Economies." Asian Development Bank, Manila, Philippines.

# 5. The Costs of (Mis)allocation of Finance: Exploring the Impact on Firms and Countries' Productivity and Growth

**Key Messages**

- **Economic and financial frictions and distortions can cause a misallocation of financial resources across firms, with significant adverse impacts on aggregate outcomes, such as productivity and growth.** At least 50 percent of the dispersion in the average product of capital within each country—a standard measure of misallocation—remains unexplained, on average, after accounting for markups and technological differences. These findings suggest a nontrivial role for potentially distortionary factors, such as financial frictions, in explaining allocative inefficiencies that dampen countries' productivity and growth.
- **Inefficiencies in finance can explain a significant fraction of the resource misallocation.** Removing financial frictions and distortions, thereby relaxing firms' financial constraints, could boost countries' productivity by up to 86 percent in middle-income countries (MICs). The largest gains are observed among countries with lower gross domestic product (GDP) per capita, with aggregate productivity gains as high as 67 percent relative to the United States.
- **In explaining differences in the levels of development across countries, it is not only the level of financial development that matters, but also whether financial resources are allocated efficiently across firms.**
- **Most of the gains from mitigating financial frictions and distortions are explained by limitations on access to finance—a scale effect—instead of the composition of the types of financing firms can access (for example, debt and equity).** The estimates show that about 65–85 percent of the misallocation of finance across firms stems from this scale effect—an inefficient allocation of the total amount of finance to firms.
- **Smaller firms face larger financial frictions and distortions, resulting in scarcity of access and a higher cost of capital when compared to larger firms.** Large productivity gains would accrue from mitigating financial frictions and distortions related to

---

This chapter draws from two background papers for this volume. Cusolito et al. (2023) explore the misallocation of finance. Muro and Castagnola (2023) analyze the linkages between the prevalence of zombie firms and insolvency systems.

firm size, thereby relaxing financial frictions for smaller firms. Although this pattern holds across all countries, it is stronger for MICs with lower GDP per capita.

- **Firm age has mixed results on firm finances across MICs and high-income countries.** In some countries, younger firms face greater scarcity of finance, whereas in other countries, younger firms account for relatively higher shares of finance than more mature firms. The firm age effect has no correlation with countries' income per capita.
- **Frictions and distortions in financial markets can prolong the survival of less-productive firms—so-called "zombie firms."** Deficiencies in insolvency systems can distort incentives—for example, supporting inefficient loan evergreening—and increase the likelihood and prolong the survival of zombie firms. Moreover, the findings show that weak insolvency systems lock up not only capital, but also labor in low-productivity uses. To the extent that labor released from exiting firms is absorbed by more productive firms, there could be significant gains in aggregate output.

## Introduction

This chapter shows that firms' financial constraints reflect inefficiencies in the allocation of capital across firms, which negatively affects aggregate outcomes such as productivity. This channel is referred to as the *between* margin in the conceptual framework presented in chapter 1. Ideally, in a well-functioning economy, financial resources flow to firms that can use them most productively, grow most rapidly, and create the most (and better) jobs. Conceptually, the returns to an additional dollar (in the form of debt or equity) should be equated across all firms, so that in equilibrium, no productivity and output gains can be reaped by taking resources from one firm and giving them to another (that is, by reallocating financial resources across firms). In reality, however, financial frictions, distortions, and market failures—such as informational asymmetry, moral hazard problems, and subsidized access to credit—exist in all countries to a greater or lesser degree. They push countries away from the ideal allocation of resources across firms, potentially leading to dispersion in the returns to capital across firms: that is, the *marginal revenue products* of these liabilities—*revenue total factor productivity* (TFPR), or as it is more commonly known, *total factor productivity* (TFP). The dispersion of marginal revenues indicates misallocation of resources. It also suggests the potential for improvements in aggregate outcomes, such as productivity gains, by reallocating financial resources across heterogeneous firms. Thus, in explaining differences in the level of development across countries, it is not only the level of financial development that matters, but also whether financial resources are allocated efficiently across firms. Box 6.1 provides an overview of the recent debate in the economics literature on the role of misallocation in aggregate outcomes.

### Is Misallocation Still Important for Productivity Growth?

Over the past 10 years, there has been a reevaluation of the importance of resource misallocation (or at least its dominance) for policy making and whether this focus on the so-called *between* margin has come at the expense of the other two margins, the *within-firm dynamics* margin and the *selection* (entry-exit) margin. The accumulated empirical results up to 2019 did not provide overwhelming support for the focus on misallocation (figure B5.1.1). Moreover, the conceptual underpinnings of the Hsieh-Klenow (2009) interpretation that dispersion in the marginal revenue product of a factor—or *total factor productivity*—uniquely captures distortions have been challenged. New evidence shows that dispersion can simply reflect markups, technological differences, or adjustment costs in capital, which vary across firms.[a,b]

Recent World Bank research by David et al. (2021) shows, however, that after accounting for markups, technological differences, adjustment costs in capital,[c] and informational asymmetries, on average, at least 50 percent of the dispersion in the average product of capital within each economy—a standard measure of misallocation—remains unexplained (figure B5.1.2). These findings suggest that there is a nontrivial role for potentially distortionary factors like financial frictions in explaining allocative inefficiencies that dampen productivity and growth. Further, this unexplained component exhibits a strong negative correlation with income per capita, indicating larger productivity gains from removing distortionary factors, especially in emerging market and developing economies.

**FIGURE B5.1.1  Which Margin Contributes More to Productivity Growth?**

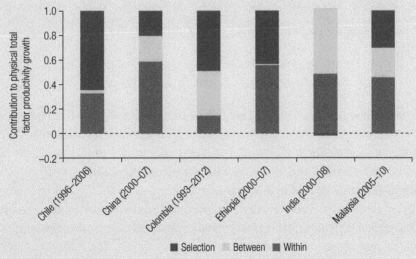

*Source:* Cusolito and Maloney 2018.
*Note:* This figure shows the contribution of each margin to productivity growth.

*(Box continues on the following page.)*

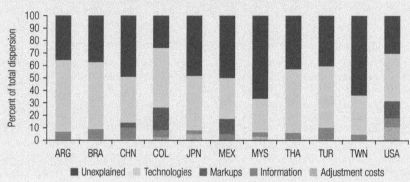
## How Does the (Mis)allocation of Finance Affect Aggregate Outcomes?

Financial liabilities (such as debt and equity) are used by firms to buy their inputs (such as energy and materials) and obtain the factors of production (labor and capital) needed to produce a good or service. Financial frictions and distortions can adversely affect TFP and output through two channels. The first one, the so-called *scale effect*, reflects changes in the gross flow of financial resources firms can obtain when frictions and distortions are present. This limitation in terms of the volume of financial resources firms can obtain constrains firms from operating at an efficient scale, expanding their production, and withstanding economic and financial shocks. The second channel, the so-called *composition effect*, reflects deviations in the debt-to-equity composition from the optimal one, given firms' production and investment plans. This constraint in terms of the type of financial resources firms can access is relevant, as highlighted in the case of financing innovation in chapter 3. Firms might retrench or abstain entirely from investments in tangible and/or intangible assets when finance is limited or unavailable, for instance.

There is now a large body of literature that focuses on identifying the drivers of misallocation of resources across firms and quantifying the productivity and output gains emerging market and developing economies (EMDEs) can obtain by removing frictions and distortions. However, most of the literature focuses on economic distortions that affect input and factor markets.[1] Little has been said about the role of financial frictions and distortions and (mis)allocation.[2] This chapter takes a step forward in filling this gap. It provides evidence of the role of the misallocation of finance for a sample of 24 European countries over 2010–16.[3] The framework adopted here is an extension of the Whited and Zhao (2021) model (see box 5.2 for details). The sections that follow shed light on the large productivity gains from removing financial frictions and distortions and reducing misallocation and which firms are the most vulnerable to the effects of these financial frictions, distortions, and (mis)allocation.

---

### BOX 5.2

**Financial Distortions, Misallocation, and Total Factor Productivity: Background Theory**

To explore the impact of finance (mis)allocation on productivity and output, Cusolito et al. (2023) rely on the framework developed by Whited and Zhao (2021), which is an extension of the static model presented by Hsieh and Klenow (2009). The latter assumes monopolistic competition in final product markets, constant returns-to-scale technology, and heterogeneous firms (with different efficiency levels and capital and output distortions). The unit of analysis is the industry. In this setting, real economic distortions disrupt the equality of the marginal revenue product of each factor (MRPF) across firms in an industry and decrease total factor productivity (TFP). The greater is the dispersion of MRPF within a sector, the greater is the level of misallocation, as well as the potential productivity gains a country can obtain from removing such economic distortions. The basic intuition is that in equilibrium, firms should have the same MRPF, and departure from this condition triggers inefficiency in the production process.

Instead of modeling the labor-capital mix that leads to distortions in TFP, as in the Hsieh-Klenow model, Whited and Zhao model the financial liabilities (such as debt and equity) that firms employ to purchase the factor mix. The Whited-Zhao model considers finance as a primitive input in the production process, which is needed to purchase the proximate factors (labor and capital) and inputs (material and energy). Moreover, while the Hsieh-Klenow model assumes that labor and capital are imperfect substitutes, the Whited-Zhao model extends the original framework by allowing different forms of finance (that is, debt and equity) to be perfect or imperfect substitutes. This extra flexibility is important because it allows for a frictionless Modigliani-Miller framework, in which firms' capital structure is irrelevant, as a baseline, and it helps in understanding whether potential reallocation gains stem from rearranging the debt-to-equity mix across firms (the *composition effect*) or from a reallocation of the gross flow of resources from less efficient to more efficient firms (the *scale effect*). In other words, at an optimal allocation, the marginal revenue products of the financial liabilities are equal across all firms in an industry. Financial frictions and distortions disrupt this equality and can adversely affect TFP through two channels. The first one, *the scale effect*, alters the gross flow of financial resources firms can obtain compared to the flow they would have obtained in a frictionless economy. The second one, *the composition effect*, causes the debt-to-equity mix to deviate from the optimal one a firm would have chosen in a frictionless economy.

## Quantifying Financial Misallocation: Scale Effects and Composition Effects

Financial frictions and distortions in debt and equity markets have a sizable impact on aggregate productivity, as measured by TFP (figure 5.1). Productivity gains from removing financial market inefficiencies—caused by financial frictions (such as those caused by information asymmetries and other market failures) or distortions (such as policy-induced ones)—range from about 16 to 86 percent. Relative to the United States, the estimated productivity gains in middle-income countries (MICs) range from 21 to 67 percent.[4]

The degree of misallocation of finance tends to vary negatively with income per capita—misallocation of finance is twice as severe between the country with the lowest GDP per capita and the country with the highest GDP per capita in the sample. In other words, countries that are far from the development frontier (with low levels of GDP per capita) would gain the most from removing financial frictions and distortions, which would trigger a reallocation of financial resources toward financially constrained yet productive firms (figure 5.2). The estimates show that the countries with lower GDP per capita in the sample are among the most affected by financial frictions and distortions, and they would be the ones that could gain the most from removing such inefficiencies. In other words, productivity gains from reducing misallocation of finance diminish along the development path.

Interestingly, the results show that constraints on access to finance (*scale effect*) rather than an inefficient allocation in debt-equity financing (*composition effect*) in large part drive this misallocation of capital across firms. The estimates show that roughly 65 to 85 percent of the gains from removing frictions and distortions and improving the allocation of financial resources across firms comes from the scale effect

**FIGURE 5.1** **Many Countries Could Reap Substantial Gains from Removing Financial Frictions and Distortions**

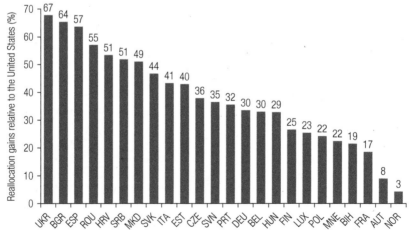

*Source:* Adapted from Cusolito et al. 2023.

*Note:* The figure shows the counterfactual aggregate total factor productivity gains that each country would enjoy if the misallocation of finance were reversed, relative to the United States. The figure uses International Organization for Standardization country codes.

Unleashing Productivity through Firm Financing

**FIGURE 5.2**  **Developing Countries Could Benefit the Most from Removing Financial Misallocation**

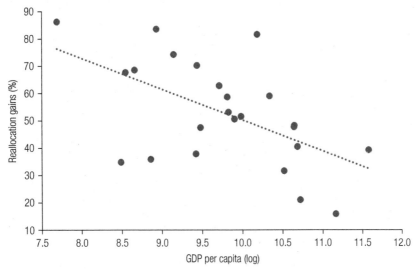

Coefficient: −17.955; T-statistic: −2.862; R-squared: 0.271

*Source:* Cusolito et al. 2023.

*Note:* The figure shows the counterfactual aggregate total factor productivity gains that each country would enjoy if the misallocation of finance were reversed. GDP = gross domestic product.

instead of the composition effect (figure 5.3). That is, removing financial market inefficiencies associated with the scale effect can lead to aggregate productivity gains of up to 73 percent in MICs. These results indicate that distortions in the gross flow of financial resources (access to financial resources) play a crucial role in real productivity and output losses due to inefficiencies in finance. These patterns reinforce the importance of access to debt finance, which constitutes the bulk of financing to firms in EMDEs, as shown in chapters 2 and 3.

Nonetheless, there is a positive correlation between the productivity gains from changing the composition of financing—arguably by improving firms' access to equity financing—and the extent of innovative activity among MICs (figure 5.4). That is, countries with more creative outputs and more knowledge and technology outputs—and thus with arguably a larger share of firms engaging in innovative activities—would benefit the most from an improvement in the allocation of capital between debt and equity. These results suggest that the composition of finance—the debt and equity mix—matters for aggregate productivity, at least in part because of the value of equity for innovative firms.

The estimations show that an inefficient allocation of financial resources explains, at least partly, allocative inefficiencies in markets for inputs (such as energy and materials) and factors of production (such as labor and capital) (figure 5.5). Box 5.3 provides corroborating evidence drawn from the World Bank Enterprise Surveys. There are two ways of interpreting this finding. The first relates to the idea that frictions

**FIGURE 5.3** **Addressing the Scale Effect Is a Greater Source of Potential TFP Gains Than Adjusting the Debt-to-Equity Composition**

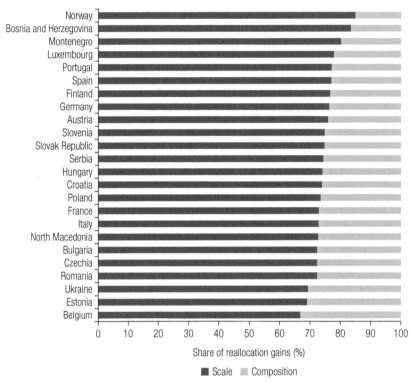

*Source:* Cusolito et al. 2023.

*Note:* The figure shows the counterfactual aggregate total factor productivity (TFP) gain for each country if the misallocation of finance was reversed under the baseline estimation of the elasticity of substitution between debt and equity and under the alternative scenario of perfect substitutability. The gains under perfect substitution are depicted in brown, and the difference between the baseline and perfect substitution, which measures the contribution of the composition effect through the debt-to-equity ratio, is depicted in orange.

**FIGURE 5.4** **Middle-Income Countries with a Larger Share of Innovative Firms Would Reap the Most Benefits from Increasing Equity Finance**

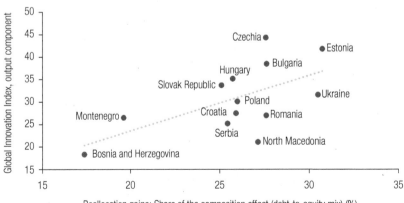

*Sources:* Calculations based on Cusolito et al. 2023; World Development Indicators; and World Intellectual Property Organization.

## FIGURE 5.5  (Mis)allocation of Finance Arguably Lies behind Input and Factor (Mis)allocation

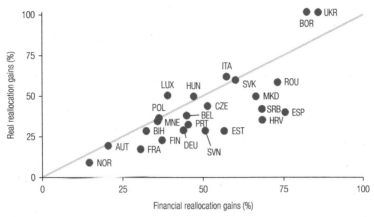

Source: Cusolito et al. 2023.

Note: The figure shows the counterfactual aggregate total factor productivity gain for each country if the misallocation of finance was reversed (x-axis, reallocation gains computed following Whited and Zhao (2021)), against the counterfactual productivity gain that would be obtained from reversing real input misallocation (y-axis, reallocation gains computed following Hsieh and Klenow (2009)). The figure also shows the 45-degree line in orange. The data labels use International Organization for Standardization country codes.

---

### BOX 5.3

### Global Productivity Gains from Improving Access to Credit

Corroborating the evidence in this chapter, Correa, Cusolito, and Pena (2019) show that the Hsieh and Klenow (2009) measures of real distortions are negatively and primarily correlated with access to finance for a sample of 68 emerging market and developing economies. The analysis is based on the World Bank Enterprise Surveys and controls for formal and informal competition; red tape; informal payments; tax-related bribes; and country, industry, and time fixed effects. The results show that restrictions in access to finance may explain the misallocation of resources in input and product markets. Importantly, removing financial frictions and distortions and improving access to credit are productivity enhancing across all geographical regions. The largest productivity gains would occur in Sub-Saharan Africa, South Asia, and the Middle East and North Africa (table B5.3.1).

### TABLE B5.3.1  Productivity Changes as a Result of Distortions in the Business Environment

| Explanatory variables | Coefficient | | Median marginal effect | | | | | | F stat. | p-value |
|---|---|---|---|---|---|---|---|---|---|---|
| | $\delta_{k1}$ | $\delta_{k2}$ | EAP | ECA | LAC | MENA | SA | SSA | | |
| Access to credit | 0.003 | 0.105 | 0.015 | 0.034 | 0.019 | 0.015 | 0.059 | 0.091 | 5.567 | 0.062 |
| Competition from informal firms | −0.205 | 0.234 | −0.256 | −0.211 | −0.245 | −0.256 | −0.151 | −0.073 | 22.811 | 0 |
| Red tape | −0.004 | −0.001 | −0.007 | −0.007 | −0.007 | −0.007 | −0.007 | −0.007 | 12.589 | 0.002 |
| Informal payments | −0.024 | 0.036 | −0.061 | −0.053 | −0.059 | −0.061 | −0.042 | −0.027 | 24.055 | 0 |
| Tax-related bribes | −0.263 | 0.035 | −0.35 | −0.342 | −0.349 | −0.35 | −0.332 | −0.318 | 20.744 | 0 |
| Product market competition | −0.004 | −0.159 | −0.022 | −0.049 | −0.028 | −0.022 | −0.087 | −0.135 | 13.593 | 0.001 |
| No. of observations | 7,505 | | | | | | | | | |
| R-squared | 0.492 | | | | | | | | | |

Source: Correa, Cusolito, and Pena 2019.

Note: This table presents estimated coefficients (linear and interaction terms with each explanatory variable) and the marginal effect of changes on firm-level productivity (measured as revenue total factor productivity). The marginal effects are evaluated for the median firm. EAP = East Asia and Pacific; ECA = Europe and Central Asia; LAC = Latin America and the Caribbean; MENA = Middle East and North Africa; SA = South Asia; SSA =Sub-Saharan Africa.

and distortions, no matter the source, mirror the fundamental and systemic problems that many EMDEs face, such as weak institutions broadly defined, including weak regulatory and institutional frameworks. Therefore, economies that display poor performance in allocating their real resources are also expected to display similar inefficiencies when allocating financial resources. The second interpretation is rooted in Whited and Zhao's (2021) argument of considering financial liabilities to be direct factor inputs for firms. By shutting down the channel of resources internal to the firm, using financial liabilities like debt and/or equity is the only way firms have to hire workers or make investments in tangible assets like capital or intangible ones like research and development. Therefore, there is a one-to-one mapping between misallocation of real and financial liabilities. That is, an inefficient allocation of financial resources across firms creates inefficiencies in real markets, as labor and capital flow to firms that face small distortions, but they are not necessarily the most productive ones.

## Financial Misallocation across Firm Size and Age

The estimations show that the misallocation of finance is particularly harmful for small firms. Smaller firms face greater scarcity of finance, and thus pay a higher cost of capital than larger firms due to financial frictions and distortions (see box 5.4 for methodological details on the identification of this effect). These results indicate that mitigating financial frictions and distortions would relax financial frictions for smaller firms and would have a sizable impact on boosting aggregate productivity.

---

### BOX 5.4

#### Identifying the Effects across Firm Size and Age

Many scholars have challenged the restrictive theoretical underpinnings underlying the Hsieh-Klenow framework (and therefore the Whited-Zhao (2021) framework)—and the derived interpretation of the dispersion of revenue total factor productivity (TFPR) as uniquely capturing distortions—as empirically unrealistic.[a] These challenges have left researchers uncertain as to what the TFPR dispersion really captures. As summarized in Cusolito and Maloney (2018), the Hsieh-Klenow framework interprets any difference across firms in TFPR as reflecting frictions and distortions, despite allowing for underlying productivity differences across firms. For this to be the case, the model needs to assume that any increase in productivity is fully offset by a fall in prices (that is, that the elasticity of prices to technological improvements = –1).

However, the empirical evidence challenges these assumptions. Analysis of firm-level census data for the United States suggests that industry-level elasticities are generally substantially less than 1, and actually closer to 0.5 or 0.6. That is, only about half of the increase in efficiency would be offset by a fall in prices, and that increase would therefore raise measured TFPR (Haltiwanger, Kulick, and Syverson 2018). Recent empirical work for emerging market and developing economies (EMDEs) has not been supportive of those assumptions either.[b] Studies for Argentina, Chile, Colombia, India, and Slovenia show incomplete pass-through. Moreover, research for Chile, Malaysia, and Mexico shows that firms with lower marginal costs produce

*(Box continues on the following page.)*

Unleashing Productivity through Firm Financing

### Identifying the Effects across Firm Size and Age *(continued)*

more output, as expected. However, they also display higher markups, thus suggesting that the pass-through is not complete.

TFPR dispersion can also mirror differences in technology and markups. The assumption that all firms have the same underlying production processes (technology) is probably too strong, as Kasahara, Nishida, and Suzuki (2017) document. Examining the Japanese knitted garment industry, they find that heterogeneity in technology accounted for approximately 20 percent of measured increases in productivity. In addition, recent work by David et al. (2021) uses firm-level Orbis data for a larger number of countries and finds that heterogeneity in firm-level technologies potentially explains between one-quarter and one-half of the dispersion in the marginal product of capital, while the dispersion of markups is generally modest.

Other key drivers of firm performance, such as adjustment costs in capital, coupled with sales volatility and quality upgrading, as well as risk and uncertainly, can also explain part of the dispersion in TFPR. For example, using firm-level data for a large sample of EMDEs, Asker, Collard-Wexler, and De Loecker (2014) show that 60 to 90 percent of calibrated TFPR dispersion is explained by adjustment costs in capital coupled with volatility in sales. TFPR dispersion can reflect quality differences across firms. Conceptually, additional price variance that is not driven by marginal costs will show up as dispersion. In addition, quality dispersion may increase with the level of quality. Krishna, Levchenko, and Maloney (2018) show that as the average standardized quality rises, so does the dispersion and total factor productivity. Last but not least, dispersion in TFPR can also reflect risk and uncertainly. As empirical support for this effect, Doraszelski and Jaumandreu (2013) show that engaging in risky innovation, such as research and development activities, roughly doubles the degree of uncertainty in the evolution of a producer's productivity level.

Thus, identifying the effects of firm size and age on the cost of capital requires teasing out the effects of technological, markup, quality, capital adjustment costs, and risk differences from the cost of capital. To do so, the Whited-Zhao model is used to obtain measures of the cost of capital—a weighted average of the cost of debt and equity—for each firm. Then, using firm-level data from Orbis, the authors calculate the cost of capital and regress it against the logarithm of assets (as a proxy for firm size), age, and physical total factor productivity. The estimations rely on the identifying assumption that these potential confounded factors are time-invariant firm characteristics, given the short period of analysis (2010–16). Therefore, the estimations also include firm fixed effects in the main specification to control for these factors. Moreover, the estimations include country and industry-time fixed effects to control for country risk and industry trends, respectively.

a. This discussion is based on Cusolito et al. (2023) and Cusolito and Maloney (2018).
b. See Chen and Juvenal (2016); Cusolito, García-Marín, and Maloney (2017); Cusolito, Iacovone, and Sanchez (2018); De Loecker et al. (2016); De Loecker and Warzynski (2012); Eslava and Haltiwanger (2017); and Zaourak (2018).

Although this finding is robust across all countries, the firm size premium decreases with GDP per capita (figures 5.6 and 5.7). That is, inefficiencies in the allocation of finance across firm size are significantly smaller in high-income countries (HICs) than in MICs. These results are consistent with the underlying assumptions and results in chapters 2 and 3.

**FIGURE 5.6  Capital Costs Are Higher for Smaller Firms across All Countries**

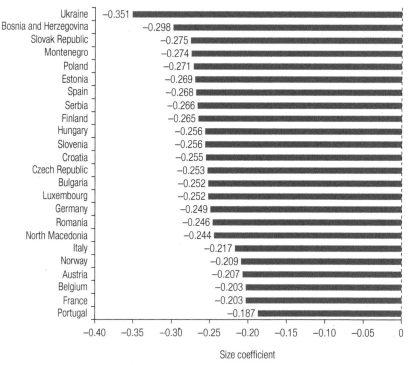

*Source:* Cusolito et al. 2023.

*Note:* The figure shows the coefficient from the regression of the model-based average cost of finance on firm size (measured by total assets), controlling for firm age, time fixed effects, and country fixed effects.

**FIGURE 5.7  The Firm Size Premium Decreases with Countries' Economic Development**

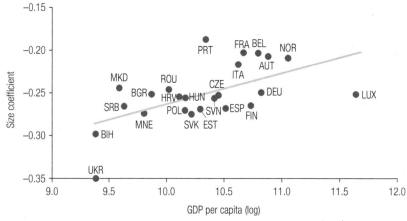

Coefficient: 0.037; T-statistic: 3.352; R-squared: 0.338

*Source:* Cusolito et al. 2023.

*Note:* This figure shows the correlation between the estimated coefficient that captures the effect of size on the average cost of capital against GDP per capita. GDP per capita is based on constant purchasing power parity from the World Bank World Development Indicators. The figure uses International Organization for Standardization country codes. GDP = gross domestic product.

Unleashing Productivity through Firm Financing

The results are also robust across all industries (figure 5.8). Interestingly, network industries, such as electricity, gas, steam, and air conditioning supply, display the lowest cost premiums (there is less scarcity of financing) associated with firm size (figure 5.9). The cost gaps between firms that are above and below the median size within an industry are relatively smaller for network industries, which exhibit lower levels of size dispersion compared to sectors such as services. This finding is probably explained by the intrinsic technological characteristics of these sectors, such as large fixed and sunk costs, that make large firms the only ones able to break even and compete in the segment. Hence, firms that are below the median size in these industries are likely larger firms and thereby less financially constrained, compared to firms that are below the median size in other sectors.

**FIGURE 5.8** **Capital Costs Are Higher for Smaller Firms across All Sectors**

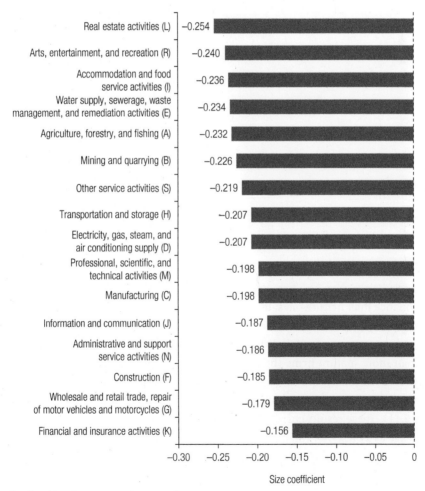

Source: Cusolito et al. 2023.

Note: The figure shows the coefficient from the regression of the model-based average cost of finance on firm size, controlling for firm age, time fixed effects, and country fixed effects. The labels show in parentheses the sectoral classification according to NACE 1. NACE = Nomenclature of Economic Activities.

FIGURE 5.9 **The Average Cost of Finance for Large and Small Firms Differs across Sectors**

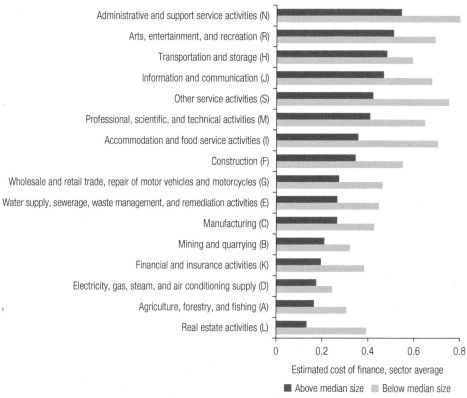

Estimated cost of finance, sector average

■ Above median size   ■ Below median size

*Source:* Cusolito et al. 2023.

*Note:* The figure shows the model-based estimated average cost of finance across firms of different sizes, across sectors. The labels show in parentheses the sectoral classification according to NACE 1. NACE = Nomenclature of Economic Activities.

The results are mixed on firm age. While on average young firms have greater scarcity of finance than mature ones, there is significant variation across countries. In some countries, mature firms have greater access to finance, whereas in other countries, younger firms account for relatively higher shares of finance and thereby face lower costs than more mature firms (figure 5.10). For example, young firms have access to cheaper finance than more mature firms in countries like Belgium, France, Norway, and Poland. The firm age premium has no correlation with countries' income per capita (figure 5.11). These results corroborate the findings in chapters 2 and 3 and cast doubt on firm age as a proxy for financial constraints on firms in EMDEs.

On differences across sectors, in network industries, mature firms face higher capital costs than young firms. However, the reverse applies for other industries (figures 5.12 and 5.13). In service sectors, such as financial services and education, where firm age proxies for experience, young firms face greater scarcity of capital.

**FIGURE 5.10**  **The Cost of Capital Is Generally Lower for Mature Firms Than Young Ones, but This Varies across Countries**

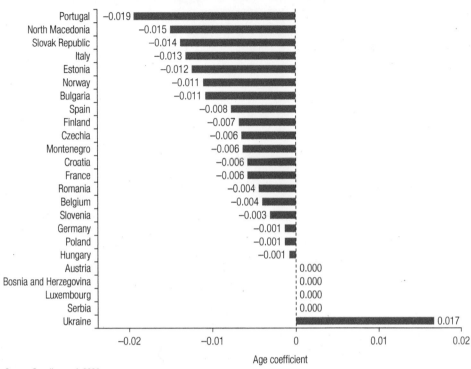

Source: Cusolito et al. 2023.

Note: The figure shows the coefficient from the regression of the model-based average cost of finance on firm age, controlling for firm size, time fixed effects, and country fixed effects.

**FIGURE 5.11**  **There Is No Correlation between the Firm Age Premium and Countries' Economic Development**

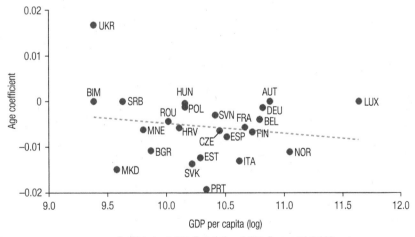

Coefficient: −0.002; T-statistic; −0.789; R-squared: 0.028

Source: Cusolito et al. 2023.

Note: The figure shows the correlation between the estimated coefficient that captures the effect of age on the average cost of capital against GDP per capita. GDP per capita is based on constant purchasing power parity from the World Bank World Development Indicators. The data labels use International Organization for Standardization country codes. GDP = gross domestic product.

The Costs of (Mis)allocation of Finance

## FIGURE 5.12   The Firm Age Premium Varies across Sectors

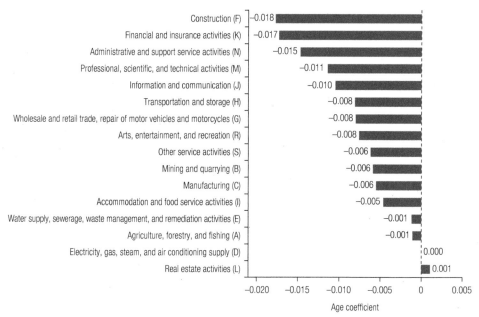

*Source:* Cusolito et al. 2023.

*Note:* The figure shows the coefficient from the regression of the model-based average cost of finance on firm age, controlling for firm size, time fixed effects, and country fixed effects. The labels show in parentheses the sectoral classification according to NACE 1. NACE = Nomenclature of Economic Activities.

## FIGURE 5.13   Young and Mature Firms Face Different Financial Costs

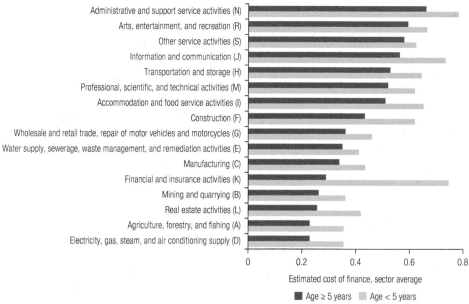

*Source:* Cusolito et al. 2023.

*Note:* The figure shows the model-based estimated average cost of finance among mature (5 years or more) and young (less than 5 years) firms across sectors. The labels show in parentheses the sectoral classification according to NACE 1. NACE = Nomenclature of Economic Activities.

## Zombie Firms, Insolvency Regimes, and Resource Misallocation

Financial frictions and distortions in debt and equity markets can also distort incentives and prolong the survival of less productive firms—the so-called "zombie firms." These are typically inefficient, debt-ridden companies with very low or even negative productivity (Caballero, Hoshi, and Kashyap 2008). The theoretical literature suggests a few channels through which the survival of zombie firms can contribute to resource misallocation, thus lowering aggregate productivity and output. First, zombie firms themselves can exhibit low levels of productivity. Second, zombie firms can crowd out investment of productive firms (undermining their productivity growth). Third, zombie firms can hinder efficient resource allocation by congesting and discouraging entry (through higher entry costs) and investments.[5] Recent studies suggest that zombie firms not only tend to invest less than non-zombie ones, but they also contribute to crowding out investment in the entire industry segment that has elevated shares of zombie firms.[6] They also prevent more productive firms from gaining market share.[7] Moreover, zombie firms can crowd out credit to healthier and more productive firms (Andrews and Petroulakis 2019). Credit misallocation favoring zombie firms can reduce the failure rate of nonviable firms while increasing it for healthy firms (Schivardi, Sette, and Tabellini 2017). Zombie firms can also limit the room for new firms to experiment with promising but uncertain technologies and business practices—further reducing the scope for within-firm productivity gains.

Research has explored the causes leading to the rise of zombie firms, highlighting two in particular: the role of the credit relationship between banks and zombie firms, and the characteristics of available exit mechanisms. On the first cause, weakly capitalized banks tend to be a key driver of extending the terms of loans to prop up zombie firms (evergreening) (Acharya et al. 2020) and even supporting increased indebtedness of zombie firms (Storz et al. 2017). Lower interest rates, in recent years, have also been shown to stave off pressure on failing firms. On the second cause, discussions about exit as an additional means of facilitating the emergence of zombie firms have, in turn, centered on insolvency systems. Although firms can exit in various ways, including by voluntarily closing their businesses, when market or financial pressures are at play, firm exit is typically channeled through the insolvency system (World Bank 2022). Stronger insolvency systems can lower failure rates for small and medium enterprises (SMEs) because they help mitigate creditors' risks by increasing their expected return in case the business is reorganized or liquidated.[8] Evidence from HICs suggests that in jurisdictions where bankruptcy legal protections are stronger, levels of entrepreneurship rise.[9]

Insolvency systems remain at the early stages of legal and regulatory maturity or rely on suboptimal institutional settings in many EMDEs (Menezes and Muro 2022). Occasionally, these systems function sufficiently poorly that debtors and creditors may use the system in a suboptimal way or become reluctant to use the system at all.

Yet, even where insolvency systems do not function perfectly, firm exit must occur, raising the question of whether alternative mechanisms, such as out-of-court workouts, can satisfy the need for business exit in an effective way. This question is particularly relevant at a juncture when the accumulation of long-term debt has raised the prospects of increased corporate vulnerabilities (Araujo et al. 2022).

A common misunderstanding surrounding the link between bankruptcy laws and employment is the idea that business failures lead to job losses. However, it is not "bankruptcy" per se that leads to job losses, but rather the process of firm exit. The role of insolvency frameworks is to create a level playing field that permits nonviable businesses to exit swiftly and predictably, thereby permitting viable businesses to restructure. In this way, insolvency frameworks can play a pivotal role in saving jobs. Moreover, to the extent that labor released from exiting firms is absorbed by more productive firms, there could be gains in aggregate output. Deficiencies in insolvency systems can distort incentives—such as supporting inefficient loan evergreening—that prolong the survival of zombie firms.

Research has started to explore the relationship between the quality of insolvency systems and the related effects on the proliferation of zombie firms. The hypothesis is that stronger insolvency legal and institutional frameworks facilitate the restructuring of viable firms and the liquidation of unviable ones, thereby reducing the number of zombie firms and promoting business dynamism. Adalet McGowan, Andrews, and Millot (2017a, 2017b) show for 14 HICs that insolvency regimes with low barriers to corporate restructuring and low personal cost to entrepreneurial failure have a lower share of capital sunk in zombie firms and are also associated with higher productivity growth of laggard firms. In the same vein, Andrews and Petroulakis (2019) show that improvements in banks' financial conditions—making them better able to absorb losses from writing off nonperforming loans—are more likely to be associated with a reduction in the prevalence of zombie firms where insolvency regimes facilitate restructuring. This section goes one step further and presents a set of results characterizing the links between zombie firm congestion and the quality of insolvency systems in a sample of MICs and HICs. Box 5.5 provides details of the methodological approach and the data used for the analysis.

The estimation results show that in MICs and HICs, as the quality of insolvency systems increases, the likelihood of zombie firms in the marketplace decreases.[10] That is, there is a negative correlation between the quality of insolvency systems and the prevalence of zombie firms. Moreover, the estimation results show that in both MICs and HICs, as the quality of a jurisdiction's insolvency system increases, the share of capital sunk in zombie firms decreases, and vice versa.[11] Estimates for MICs indicate that a one-point increase in the index capturing the strength of the insolvency framework is associated with a 1 percent reduction of the zombie capital share (figure 5.14).

## Data for the Analysis of the Prevalence of Zombie Firms

The analysis is this section is focused on firm-level data on private firms from 2014 to 2016 in 40 high-income countries and middle-income countries.[a] The data source is Bureau van Dijk's Orbis global data set, which is described in chapter 2. In addition to the data cleaning steps taken, for the purposes of the analysis here, key additional steps focused on: (1) excluding agriculture and farming (as in Baliamoune-Lutz and Lutz 2018); (2) excluding inactive firms, firms undergoing bankruptcy, and firms that had used some form of bankruptcy (as in Adalet McGowan, Andrews, and Millot 2017a, 2017b); and (3) concentrating on large firms—those with 250 or more employees or more than €43 million in total assets (as in Storz et al. 2017). The results in this chapter focus on countries with at least 1,000 firms in the cleaned data set.

Previous research has proposed different ways to assess whether a firm is a zombie.[b] One method concentrates on whether an unprofitable firm receives financing at market value. In this case, zombie firms are identified as those receiving subsidized credit. Another method focuses on a firm's financial standing and defines a firm as a zombie when its interest coverage ratio is less than 1 for a certain period of time, such as at least three consecutive years. Yet another method looks not at financial distress, but rather at solvency. A firm whose assets are insufficient to cover the existing debt is considered a zombie. Lastly, a more conservative approach considers firms to be zombies only when their financial distress has led then to a solvency problem.

Data limitations lead to the choice of this last option for the purposes of this section. This conservative approach likely undercounts the total number of zombie firms in a given country, only finding the more extreme ones.[c] In turn, this is an advantage for this study because the measure chosen is typically used in insolvency systems around the world to allow for the initiation of reorganization or liquidation procedures, and its assessment is considered best international practice.[d,e] Once zombie firms were identified for 2016, the main variable of interest, the *zombie capital share*, was constructed by aggregating the capital stock across zombie firms within each industry for each country.[f] The analysis is thus conducted at the country-industry level.

a. This box is based on Muro and Castagnola (2023), a background paper for this volume.
b. In studies with public firms, researchers have looked at growth opportunities, defining a firm as a zombie if the market value of the company divided by the replacement cost of its assets (Tobin's Q) is below the median within its sector in any given year. See, for example, Banerjee and Hofmann (2018).
c. Given that more robust insolvency systems help to adjust nonperforming loan levels faster (Carcea et al. 2015), the undercount is likely more pronounced in countries with weaker insolvency systems.
d. See, for example, Article 11 of the Serbian Bankruptcy Law and Article 2 of the Law of the People's Republic of China on Enterprise Bankruptcy.
e. See the World Bank Principles for Effective Insolvency and Creditor/Debtor Rights (World Bank 2021).
f. The analysis follows the same steps as Adalet McGowan, Andrews, and Millot (2017a, 2017b) to construct the dependent variable, but uses the debt-to-assets ratio as the criterion for identifying a zombie firm, rather than the interest coverage ratio.

In addition, larger companies are less likely to be zombies. The tangibility of assets also has a similar relationship to the likelihood of a firm being a zombie, highlighting the importance of asset-based lending for insolvent or near insolvent firms. Overall, these results further support theoretical predictions on the effect of weak insolvency systems on the prevalence of zombie firms.

**FIGURE 5.14** **As the Quality of a Jurisdiction's Insolvency System Increases, the Share of Capital Sunk in Zombie Firms Decreases**

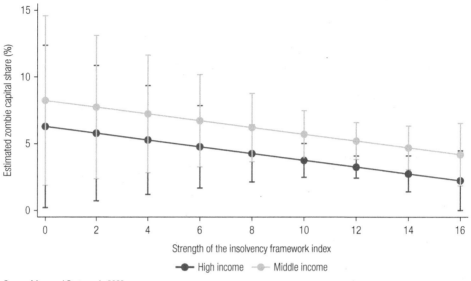

Source: Muro and Castagnola 2023.

Note: The figure shows the estimated average share and confidence intervals at 95 percent.

The estimations for MICs show that weak insolvency systems are associated with misallocation of not only capital, but also employment, as captured by the within-industry share of employment in zombie firms. That is, weak insolvency systems are associated with a higher prevalence of zombie firms, which lock up not only capital, but also labor in low productivity uses. The effects of the zombie phenomenon on business dynamism can also be observed in terms of job creation. Sectors with stronger zombie firm growth have been shown to depress job creation (Acharya et al. 2020; Caballero, Hoshi, and Kashyap 2008), a phenomenon affecting both zombie and non-zombie firms in those sectors. Relatedly, recent work suggests that industries with above average levels of zombie firms tend to experience below average growth in labor productivity and employment (Adalet McGowan et al. 2018). Stifling investment and capital reallocation can thus in turn lower productivity growth.

## Conclusions

The growth literature over the past few decades has placed the issue of resource misallocation at center stage as an explanation for differences in income across countries. Recent evidence has confirmed the relevance of the agenda for EMDEs. While most of the academic and policy discussion has centered around the role of frictions and distortions that affect input and factor markets, this chapter emphasized the role of financial frictions and distortions in financial markets—the misallocation of finance.

In particular, the chapter provided evidence indicating that firms' financial constraints reflect inefficiencies in the allocation of capital across firms (the between margin in the framework presented in chapter 2), and these inefficiencies negatively affect aggregate outcomes, such as productivity and growth.

Four key findings emerged from the analysis. First, removing financial frictions and distortions can yield large productivity gains, and these gains tend to be higher for countries with lower levels of income per capita. Second, constraints in access to finance (scale effect), rather than an inefficient allocation in the mix of debt and equity financing (composition effect), in large part drive this misallocation of capital across firms. The results also suggest that the composition of finance matters for aggregate productivity, at least in part because of the value of equity for innovative firms. Third, smaller firms face larger distortions than larger firms and, therefore, have more limited access to financial resources. Hence, larger productivity gains would accrue for smaller firms than for larger firms from a reallocation of financial resources toward financially constrained yet productive firms. Importantly, these gains also diminish with income levels. That is, developing countries would benefit the most from a more efficient allocation of finance toward smaller firms. Fourth, weak insolvency systems are associated with a higher prevalence of zombie firms, which lock up not only capital, but also labor in low productivity uses. The results in this chapter indicate that robust insolvency systems can free up capital and labor to be applied toward more productive uses.[12] This is particularly important during the recovery from the COVID-19 pandemic, at a time when corporate debt in developing economies has nearly doubled and many firms face risks stemming from debt overhang (Menezes and Muro 2022).

The novel findings in this chapter provide strong analytical underpinnings for existing, practical knowledge in supporting financing for SMEs. The results show that improving access to finance for smaller firms would help them to overcome financial constraints, thereby supporting efficiency gains and increasing productivity. These productivity gains can be sizable especially in developing countries. The results also highlight the importance of supporting access to debt finance for firms, as the misallocation of finance across firms stems in large part from a scale effect, and debt is typically the main source of financing for firms in EMDEs, as suggested in chapters 2 and 3. Nonetheless, equity financing also matters. For instance, countries with more innovative activities could obtain sizable productivity gains from rebalancing the composition of financing to firms, improving firms' access to equity finance. Last but not least, strengthening insolvency systems to facilitate the exit of zombie firms is key for fostering the reallocation of both financial resources and labor toward more efficient uses.

Although the findings suggest a roadmap in terms of policy reforms aimed at improving the allocation of financial resources across firms, evidence-based policies that account for individual country context are paramount. As the results in this chapter highlight, there is significant cross-country variation in the extent of misallocation of financial resources. Importantly, limited cross-country, firm-level data on firm financing significantly constrained the scope of the analysis in this chapter, including a wider coverage of EMDEs. This puts a premium on improving the availability of and access to granular, firm-level data, which are key for identifying the specific types of financial frictions and distortions that hinder productivity and growth. Chapter 7 delves into the policy implications of the findings in more detail, focusing on a discussion of the role of financial sector policies in unlocking the constraints in firm financing and boosting productivity and growth.

## Notes

1. The literature focuses on adjustment costs in labor and capital (Hopenhayn and Rogerson 1993), taxes (Guner, Ventura, and Xu 2008), informality (Busso, Madrigal, and Pagés 2013), government regulations (Brandt, Tombe, and Zhu 2013; Fajgelbaum et al. 2015; Hsieh and Moretti 2015), property rights (Besley and Ghatak 2010; Deininger and Feder 2001), trade protection (Pavcnik 2002; Trefler 2004), and financial frictions (Buera, Kaboski, and Shin 2011; Midrigan and Xu 2014), to mention a few.

2. Early work by Buera, Kaboski, and Shin (2011) shows that financial frictions distort the allocation of capital and entrepreneurial talent across production units and decrease aggregate/sector-level TFP. Sectors with larger scales of operation have more financing needs and are hence disproportionately vulnerable to financial distortions. Related work by Midrigan and Xu (2014) shows that financial frictions distort firms' decisions to enter a market and/or adopt technology. They also generate capital misallocation and thus productivity losses. However, both papers provide calibrated dynamic models instead of empirical firm-level evidence. Whited and Zhao's (2021) important contribution to this literature extends the Hsieh-Klenow (2009) framework to estimate real losses from misallocation of financial liabilities in China and the United States, using manufacturing firm-level data. The authors find that Chinese productivity gains from reducing financial misallocation to the US level would vary between 51 and 69 percent in terms of real value added, with only 17 to 21 percent stemming from inefficient debt-equity combinations.

3. Data limitations prevented a more comprehensive sample of countries for the analysis. See Cusolito et al. (2023) for further details.

4. These estimates compare the productivity gains for the countries in the sample with the estimation in Whited and Zhao (2021) for the United States. The authors estimated that the unadjusted gains would be 11.5 percent for the United States.

5. See, for example, Adalet McGowan et al. (2018) for an analysis of 13 Organisation for Economic Co-operation and Development countries.

6. See, for example, Banerjee and Hofmann (2018, 2020).

7. See, for example, Aghion et al. (2019); Andrews and Petroulakis (2019); Caballero, Hoshi, and Kashyap (2008); and Cooper, Haltiwanger, and Power (1997).

8. See, for example, Dewaelheyns and van Hulle (2008) and Rodano, Serrano-Velarde, and Tarantino (2012).

9. See, for example, Carcea et al. (2015); Fan and White (2003); Mathur (2009); and Peng, Yamakawa, and Lee (2010).

10. The firm-level estimations control for several firm-specific as well as country-specific characteristics: firm size (proxied by the value of total assets and the number of employees); age of the firm

measured as years since incorporation (using both levels and a quadratic term); asset tangibility, a dummy variable for small firms (those with 100 or fewer employees); an MIC dummy; the lending interest rate to capture the cost of bank financing; and the depth of the banking sector, proxied by domestic credit to the private sector as a share of GDP.

11. The reported results are robust to a number of alternative definitions of what characterizes a zombie firm. While the measure of zombie firms adopted here is largely in line with insolvency legislation across MICs and HICs, it is possible that it may fail to capture zombie firms that are not yet technically underwater, especially because a zombie firm's performance tends to deteriorate several years before zombification. Conversely, it may classify too many firms as zombies—for instance, because accounting asset valuations are artificially depressed. Hence, two alternative definitions were considered: a more conservative one in case of overidentification of zombie firms, and a less restrictive one in case of under-identification of zombie firms. The estimated results are qualitatively similar to the reported ones.

12. Robust insolvency systems can also facilitate increased access to finance, foster higher entrepreneurship levels, and support faster resolution of nonperforming loans. See, for example, Davydenko and Franks (2006); Carcea et al. (2015); and Consolo, Malfa, and Pierluigi (2018).

## References

Acharya, V. V., M. Crosignani, T. Eisert, and C. Eufinger. 2020. "Zombie Credit and (Dis-) Inflation: Evidence from Europe." Working Paper 27158, National Bureau of Economic Research, Cambridge, MA.

Adalet McGowan, M., D. Andrews, and V. Millot. 2017a. "Insolvency Regimes, Zombie Firms and Capital Reallocation." OECD Economics Department Working Paper 1399, Organisation for Economic Co-operation and Development, Paris.

Adalet McGowan, M., D. Andrews, and V. Millot. 2017b. "Insolvency Regimes, Technology Diffusion and Productivity Growth: Evidence from Firms in OECD Countries." OECD Economics Department Working Paper 1425, Organisation for Economic Co-operation and Development, Paris.

Adalet McGowan, M., D. Andrews, V. Millot, and T. Beck. 2018. "The Walking Dead? Zombie Firms and Productivity Performance in OECD Countries." *Economic Policy* 33 (96): 685–736.

Aghion, P., A. Bergeaud, T. Boppart, P. J. Klenow, and H. Li. 2019. "Missing Growth from Creative Destruction." *American Economic Review* 109 (8): 2795–2822.

Andrews, D., and F. Petroulakis. 2019. "Breaking the Shackles: Zombie Firms, Weak Banks and Depressed Restructuring in Europe." ECB Working Paper 2240, European Central Bank, Frankfurt.

Araujo, J., J. Garrido, E. Kopp, R. Varghese, and W. Yao. 2022. "Policy Options for Supporting and Restructuring Firms Hit by the COVID-19 Crisis." Strategy, Policy, and Review Department, International Monetary Fund, Washington, DC.

Asker, J., A. Collard-Wexler, and J. De Loecker. 2014. "Dynamic Inputs and Resource (Mis)Allocation." *Journal of Political Economy* 122 (5): 1013–63.

Baliamoune-Lutz, M., and S. Lutz. 2018. "International Ownership and Firm Performance in Africa." http://dx.doi.org/10.2139/ssrn.3626099.

Banerjee, R., and B. Hofmann. 2018. "The Rise of Zombie Firms: Causes and Consequences." *BIS Quarterly Review* September 2018: 67–78.

Banerjee, R., and B. Hofmann. 2020. "Corporate Zombies: Anatomy and Life Cycle." BIS Working Paper 882, Bank for International Settlements, Basel.

Besley, T., and M. Ghatak. 2010. "Property Rights and Economic Development." In *Handbook of Development and Economics*, vol. 5, edited by D. Rodrik and M. Rosenzwieg, 4525–95. New York: Elsevier.

Brandt, L., T. Tombe, and X. Zhu. 2013. "Factor Market Distortions across Time, Space, and Sectors in China." *Review of Economic Dynamics* 16 (1): 39–58.

Buera, F. J., J. P. Kaboski, and Y. Shin. 2011. "Finance and Development: A Tale of Two Sectors." *American Economic Review* 101 (5): 1964–2002.

Busso, M., L. Madrigal, and C. Pagés. 2013. "Productivity and Resource Misallocation in Latin America." *BE Journal of Macroeconomics* 13 (1): 903–32.

Caballero, J., T. Hoshi, and A. Kashyap. 2008. "Zombie Lending and Depressed Restructuring in Japan." *American Economic Review* 98 (5): 1943–77.

Carcea, M. C., D. Ciriaci, D. Lorenzani, P. Pontuch, and C. Cuerpo. 2015. "The Economic Impact of Rescue and Recovery Frameworks in the EU." European Economy Discussion Paper 2015-004, Directorate General Economic and Financial Affairs, European Commission, Brussels.

Chen, L., and N. Juvenal. 2016. "Quality, Trade, and Exchange Rate Pass-Through." *Journal of International Economics* 100 (May): 61–80.

Consolo, A., F. Malfa, and B. Pierluigi. 2018. "Insolvency Frameworks and Private Debt: An Empirical Investigation." Working Paper 2189, European Central Bank, Frankfurt.

Cooper, R., J. Haltiwanger, and L. Power. 1997. "Machine Replacement and the Business Cycle: Lumps and Bumps." NBER Working Paper 5260, National Bureau of Economic Research, Cambridge, MA.

Correa, P. G., A. P. Cusolito, and J. Pena. 2019. "Business-Environment Distortions and Firm-Level Productivity: Global Evidence." World Bank, Washington, DC.

Cusolito, A. P., R. N. Fattal-Jaef, D. S. Mare, and A. V. Singh. 2023. "From Financing to Real Misallocation: Evidence from a Global Sample." Background paper for this volume. World Bank, Washington, DC.

Cusolito, A. P., A. García-Marín, and W. F. Maloney. 2017. "Competition, Innovation, and Within-Plant Productivity: Evidence from Chilean Plants." Background paper for *Productivity Revisited: Shifting Paradigms in Analysis and Policy*, by A. P. Cusolito and W. F. Maloney. Washington, DC: World Bank.

Cusolito, A. P., L. Iacovone, and L. Sanchez. 2018. "The Effects of Chinese Competition on All the Margins of Firm Growth." Background paper for *Productivity Revisited: Shifting Paradigms in Analysis and Policy*, by A. P. Cusolito and W. F. Maloney. Washington, DC: World Bank.

Cusolito, A. P., and W. F. Maloney. 2018. *Productivity Revisited: Shifting Paradigms in Analysis and Policy*. Washington, DC: World Bank.

David, J. M., V. Venkateswaran, A. P. Cusolito, and T. Didier. 2021. "Capital Allocation in Developing Countries." *World Bank Economic Review* 35 (4): 1102–21.

Davydenko, S. A., and J. R. Franks. 2006. "Do Bankruptcy Codes Matter? A Study of Defaults in France, Germany, and the U.K." *Journal of Finance* 63 (2): 565–608.

De Loecker, J., P. Goldberg, A. Khandelwal, and N. Pavcnik. 2016. "Prices, Markups, and Trade Reform." *Econometrica* 84 (2): 2437–71.

De Loecker, J., and F. Warzynski. 2012. "Markups and Firm-Level Export Status." *American Economic Review* 102 (6): 2437–71.

Deininger, K., and G. Feder. 2001. "Land Institutions and Land Markets." In *Handbook of Agricultural Economics*, edition 1, vol. 1A, *Agricultural Production*, edited by B. L. Gardner and G. C. Rausser, 287–331. New York: Elsevier.

Dewaelheyns, N., and C. van Hulle. 2008. "Legal Reform and Aggregate Small and Micro Business Bankruptcy Rates: Evidence from the 1997 Belgian Bankruptcy Code." *Small Business Economics* 31: 409–24.

Doraszelski, U., and J. Jaumandreu. 2013. "R&D and Productivity: Estimating Endogenous Productivity." *Review of Economic Studies* 80 (4): 1338–83.

Eslava, M., and J. Haltiwanger. 2017. "The Drivers of Life-Cycle Business Growth." Background paper for *Productivity Revisited: Shifting Paradigms in Analysis and Policy*, by A. P. Cusolito and W. F. Maloney. Washington, DC: World Bank.

Fajgelbaum, P. D., E. Morales, J. C. S. Serrato, and O. M. Zaidar. 2015. "State Taxes and Spatial Misallocation." NBER Working Paper 21760, National Bureau of Economic Research, Cambridge, MA.

Fan, W., and M. J. White. 2003. "Personal Bankruptcy and the Level of Entrepreneurial Activity." *Journal of Law and Economics* 46 (2): 543–67.

Guner, N., G. Ventura, and Y. Xu. 2008. "Macroeconomic Implications of Size-Dependent Policies." *Review of Economic Dynamics* 11 (4): 721–44.

Haltiwanger, J., R. Kulick, and C. Syverson. 2018. "Misallocation Measures: The Distortion That Ate the Residual." NBER Working Paper 24199, National Bureau of Economic Research, Cambridge, MA.

Hopenhayn, H., and R. Rogerson. 1993. "Job Turnover and Policy Evaluation: A General Equilibrium Analysis." *Journal of Political Economy* 101 (5): 915–38.

Hsieh, C. T., and P. J. Klenow. 2009."Misallocation and Manufacturing TFP in China and India." *Quarterly Journal of Economics* 124 (4): 1403–48.

Hsieh, C. T., and E. Moretti. 2015. "Housing Constraints and Spatial Misallocation." NBER Working Paper 21154, National Bureau of Economic Research, Cambridge, MA.

Kasahara, H., M. Nishida, and M. Suzuki. 2017. "Decomposition of Aggregate Productivity Growth with Unobserved Heterogeneity." Discussion Paper 17083, Research Institute of Economy, Trade and Industry, Tokyo.

Krishna, P., A. Levchenko, and W. Maloney. 2018. "Growth and Risk: The View from International Trade." Background paper for *Productivity Revisited: Shifting Paradigms in Analysis and Policy*, by A. P. Cusolito and W. F. Maloney. Washington, DC: World Bank.

Mathur, A. 2009. "A Spatial Model of the Impact of Bankruptcy Law on Entrepreneurship." *Spatial Economic Analysis* 4 (1): 25–51.

Menezes, A., and S. Muro. 2022. "Addressing Insolvency Risk through Corporate Debt Restructuring Frameworks." In *Addressing the Corporate Debt Overhang*. Washington, DC: World Bank Group.

Midrigan, V., and D. Y. Xu. 2014. "Finance and Misallocation: Evidence from Plant-Level Data." *American Economic Review* 104 (2): 422–58.

Muro, S., and A. Castagnola. 2023. "Insolvency Systems and Zombie Firm Proliferation in High- and Middle-Income Economies." Background paper for this volume. World Bank, Washington, DC.

Pavcnik, N. 2002. "Trade Liberalization, Exit, and Productivity Improvement: Evidence from Chilean Plants." *Review of Economic Studies* 69 (1): 245–76.

Peng, M. W., Y. Yamakawa, and S. Lee. 2010. "Bankruptcy Laws and Entrepreneur-Friendliness." *Entrepreneurship Theory and Practice* 34 (3): 517–30.

Rodano, G., N. Serrano-Velarde, and E. Tarantino. 2012. "Bankruptcy Law and the Cost of Banking Finance." Working Paper 12/18, Oxford University Centre for Business Taxation, SAID Business School, Oxford, UK.

Schivardi, F., E. Sette, and G. Tabellini. 2017. "Credit Misallocation during the European Financial Crisis." Working Paper 1139, Bank of Italy, Rome.

Storz, M., M. Koetter, R. Setzer, and A. Westphal. 2017. "Do We Want These Two to Tango? On Zombie Firms and Stressed Banks in Europe." IWH Discussion Paper 13/2017, Halle Institute for Economic Research, Halle, Germany.

Trefler, D. 2004. "The Long and Short of the Canada-US Free Trade Agreement." *American Economic Review* 94 (4): 870–95.

Whited, T. M., and J. Zhao. 2021. "The Misallocation of Finance." *Journal of Finance* 76 (5): 2359–407.

World Bank. 2021. *Principles for Effective Insolvency and Creditor/Debtor Regimes, 2021 Edition.* Washington, DC: World Bank.

World Bank. 2022. *World Development Report 2022: Finance for Equitable Recovery.* Washington, DC: World Bank.

Zaourak, G. 2018. "Upgrading over the Life Cycle: Evidence for Malaysia." Background paper for *Productivity Revisited: Shifting Paradigms in Analysis and Policy*, by A. P. Cusolito and W. F. Maloney. Washington, DC: World Bank.

# 6. The Impact of Financial Constraints on Firms' Resilience to Shocks

---

**Key Messages**

- **Financial constraints not only can hinder the productivity and growth of firms, but can also constrain firms' ability to cope with adverse shocks.** New evidence shows that during the COVID-19 pandemic, firms in emerging market and developing economies (EMDEs) that had access to financing were better able to maintain employment levels and avoid falling into arrears.
- **Small firms were particularly vulnerable to the economic repercussions imposed by the COVID-19 pandemic, at least in part due to their limited access to finance in the first place.** Among private firms, smaller ones had the highest probability of being financially constrained during the COVID-19 pandemic. In contrast, younger firms had roughly similar probabilities of being financially constrained as more mature firms.
- **Public support programs in EMDEs aimed at mitigating firms' liquidity problems were not as effective as expected in reaching financially constrained firms.** The survey data explored in this chapter show that financially constrained firms were less likely to have access to public support across large, medium, and small firms. Moreover, larger firms were more likely to receive support across all types of support measures.
- **Access to diversified sources of financing can also help firms to weather shocks.** Capital market financing can replace bank lending during banking crises, when capital markets might act as a "spare tire," allowing firms to lessen the adverse effects of the banking crisis on performance and employment.

## Introduction

Financial constraints can hinder the productivity and growth of firms as well as constrain firms' ability to cope with adverse shocks. Access to finance for firms in emerging market and developing economies (EMDEs) is a major constraint on business operations and has an impact on firms' investments in productive capabilities, productivity, and growth during normal times, as other chapters in this volume have shown. Financing constraints can become an even bigger challenge during turbulent times. For example, Chen and Lee (2020) estimate that the tightening of credit market conditions during the global financial crisis of 2008–09, coupled with limited credit market access—especially for micro, small, and medium

---

This chapter draws from Farazi and Lopez-Cordova (2023), a background paper for this volume.

enterprises (MSMEs)—contributed to a large gap in total factor productivity between MSMEs and large firms at least until 2015. Lack of access to finance during turbulent times has also been shown to adversely affect other firm-level outcomes: employment (Chodorow-Reich 2014), with greater declines in employment in small firms than in large firms (Siemer 2019); output, capital, and patenting, as shown for a sample of German firms (Huber 2018); and product innovation (Granja and Moreira 2023). These studies also point out that the impact is typically more acute for smaller and younger firms. Most of the existing research focuses on high-income countries (HICs) and tends to draw from the global financial crisis of 2008–09 to analyze the impact of shocks on firm outcomes due to changes in their access to finance or the degree of financing constraints they faced.[1]

This chapter explores these issues in the context of the COVID-19 pandemic—a unique shock to the extent that its roots were exogenous to both the financial sector and the firms themselves. Moreover, the pandemic was an exogenous shock characterized by significant uncertainty about its magnitude and duration.[2] The COVID-19 pandemic hit firms worldwide as a powerful and damaging combination of concomitant supply shocks (notably, employees could not go to work, which in turn impaired production, disrupted supply chains, and froze investments) and demand shocks (households and firms reduced their demand for certain goods and services).[3] These shocks led to a synchronized collapse of economic activity, bringing it to a near halt at the onset of the pandemic and leading to a sluggish recovery since then.

The adverse impacts of these combined shocks on firms have been unprecedented. They led to a sudden collapse in corporate revenues, corporate cash flows plummeted to an unparalleled extent, and firms struggled to survive as their working capital was depleted. A large number of firms thus faced a severe cash crunch as the combined shocks reduced their capacity to meet their operating expenses. The liquidity shock turned into insolvency and bankruptcy for many firms that would otherwise have been viable. Hence, the economic repercussions imposed by the pandemic on firms, including the destruction of productive capacities, could have large effects on the growth prospects of HICs and EMDEs alike, not only in the short term but over the long term—especially if this destruction has affected firms that were previously more productive. Access to finance in such a context can help firms weather the shock by ensuring that they remain liquid and able to allocate resources efficiently as needed.

This chapter analyzes data from the World Bank's COVID-19 Business Pulse Survey (BPS), which was rolled out in 34 countries after the onset of the pandemic, to study whether firms that had access to finance were in a better position to overcome the pandemic shock compared to financially constrained firms.[4] Specifically, the chapter provides evidence on: (1) which firms faced financing constraints during the pandemic, (2) how firm performance was affected by limited access to finance, and (3) the outreach of the relief support programs, expanding on the findings of Cirera et al. (2021). The chapter also draws from evidence from banking crises for a brief discussion of the importance for firms of having access to diversified sources of financing as a mechanism to manage risks.

## Financial Constraints during the COVID-19 Pandemic

For the purposes of this chapter, financially constrained firms (FCFs) during the COVID-19 pandemic are defined as those hit by a sharp fall in demand and that had limited resources of their own and limited or no access to external resources and/or financing to cover operating costs and/or financial obligations.[5] This definition focuses on firms facing liquidity constraints, driven for instance by a sudden collapse in sales, which made it difficult for them to cover wage expenses, pay suppliers, and/or meet other financial obligations. Conversely, firms are considered not financially constrained if they had access to external resources to cover obligations or faced only a moderate decline in sales.

The shock brought on by the COVID-19 pandemic did not affect all firms equally: the likelihood of financial constraints across firms and across countries varied considerably (figure 6.1, panel a). FCFs were more prevalent in countries with lower gross domestic product (GDP) per capita (panel b) and, to a lesser extent, in countries with more developed financial sectors as proxied by domestic credit to the private sector (panel c). That is, across countries, there was a negative correlation between the average share of financially constrained firms in a given country and the level of development of its financial sector. The probability that a firm was financially constrained after the onset of the pandemic, according to the definition adopted here, was 19.4 percent on average across all firms in the sample. At the country level, however, the average probability ranged from nearly 77 percent in Mongolia and 56 percent in Brazil to less than 3 percent in Chile.

Although there was substantial heterogeneity across firms, smaller (but not younger) firms were more likely to be financially constrained (figure 6.2). First, larger firms were less likely to have been affected by liquidity problems than their smaller counterparts (panel a). At one extreme, firms with 100 or more workers had an 11.2 percent probability of being financially constrained, whereas for microenterprises with four or fewer workers, the probability jumped to about 21.8 percent. Second, firms in the service sector, which was the hardest hit by the pandemic, were significantly more likely to be financially constrained, with about 21.6 percent probability of being an FCF, compared to around 19.3 percent for manufacturing or retail firms (panel b). Third, exporters (about 15.4 percent probability of being an FCF) were less affected by liquidity problems than nonexporting firms (20 percent), possibly because access to foreign markets mitigated the demand shock or because exporters tended to have better access to finance (panel c). Fourth, there were no marked differences across firms' age or gender of the owner (panel c). Established firms, 15 years or older, were only slightly less likely to have been affected by liquidity problems than younger firms—about 18.3 percent versus 21 percent, respectively. On gender, both men-led and women-led firms had about the same 20 percent chance of being FCFs.

**FIGURE 6.1** **Financially Constrained Firms Are More Prevalent in Countries with Lower GDP per Capita and in Countries with Less Developed Financial Sectors**

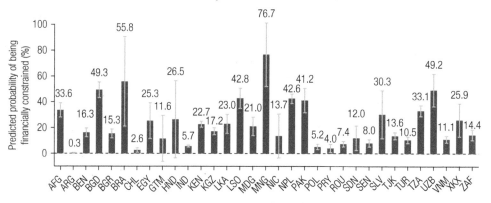

a. Financially constrained firms across countries

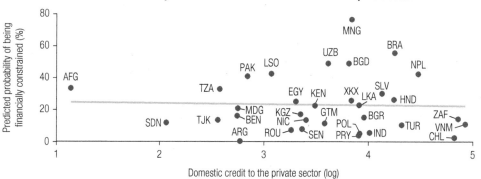

b. Financially constrained firms and domestic credit to the private sector

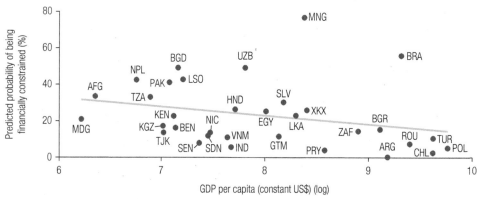

c. Financially constrained firms and GDP per capita

*Source:* Farazi and Lopez-Cordova 2023.

*Note:* Financially constrained firms are defined as those that have suffered a drop in sales of at least 30 percent during the 30 days before the survey was administered and faced any form of difficulty accessing finance, according to the World Bank COVID-19 Business Pulse Surveys. The figure shows the estimated averages across countries. Probit estimates control for sector and severity of shock brought on by the pandemic in a given country at the time of the survey. In panel a, the orange brackets show the 95 percent confidence intervals around the point estimates. The figure uses International Organization for Standardization country codes. GDP = gross domestic product.

Unleashing Productivity through Firm Financing

**FIGURE 6.2** **Smaller Firms, Firms in the Service Sector, and Nonexporters Were More Likely to Be Financially Constrained**

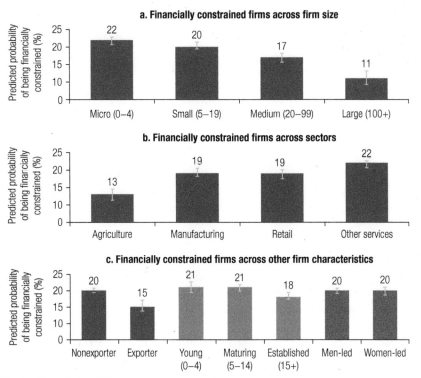

a. Financially constrained firms across firm size

b. Financially constrained firms across sectors

c. Financially constrained firms across other firm characteristics

*Source:* Farazi and Lopez-Cordova 2023.

*Note:* Financially constrained firms are defined as those that have suffered a drop in sales of at least 30 percent during the 30 days before the survey was administered and faced any form of difficulty accessing finance, according to the World Bank COVID-19 Business Pulse Surveys. The figure shows the estimated averages. Probit estimates control for country, sector, and severity of the shock brought on by the pandemic in a given country at the time of the survey. The orange brackets show the 95 percent confidence intervals around the point estimates. In panel a, micro, small, medium, and large refer to the number of employees. In panel c, young, maturing, and established refer to years in operation.

These results are supported by regression estimates of a multivariate linear probability model (figure 6.3). Interestingly, the estimates indicate that there is a monotonic decrease in the probability of being an FCF as firm size increases. The results on firm age are mixed, although the estimates show that young firms were not significantly different from established firms in terms of financial access, after controlling for a wide range of firm attributes. These estimates also show no statistically significant difference among men-led or women-led firms.[6]

## How Did Financial Constraints Affect Firm Performance?

Firms that had access to financing were better able to mitigate the adverse impact of the pandemic than financially constrained firms (figure 6.4). FCFs were more likely than firms that were not financially constrained (unconstrained firms) to adjust to the pandemic shock on the intensive margin—that is, by cutting working hours,

FIGURE 6.3 **Firm Size Is the Most Important Determinant of Being Financially Constrained**

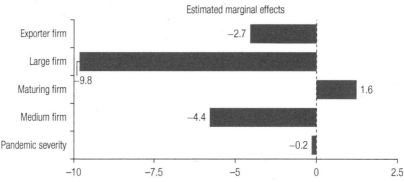

Source: Farazi and Lopez-Cordova 2023.

Note: Financially constrained firms are defined as those that have suffered a drop in sales of at least 30 percent during the 30 days before the survey was administered and faced any form of difficulty accessing finance, according to the World Bank COVID-19 Business Pulse Surveys. The figure shows the estimated averages. Probit estimates control for country, sector, and severity of the shock brought on by the pandemic in a given country at the time of the survey. "Maturing firm" refers to firms' years in operation (5–14 years).

**FIGURE 6.4** **Financially Constrained Firms Were More Likely to Cut Working Hours, Reduce Wages, Fire Workers, and Fall into Arrears than Firms That Were Not Financially Constrained**

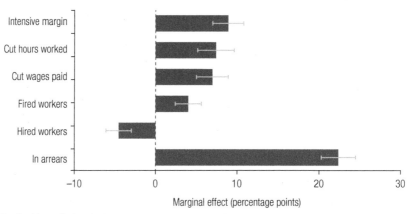

Source: Farazi and Lopez-Cordova 2023.

Note: Financially constrained firms are defined as those that have suffered a drop in sales of at least 30 percent during the 30 days before the survey was administered and that faced any form of difficulty accessing finance, according to the World Bank COVID-19 Business Pulse Surveys. The figure reports the average marginal effect that being financially constrained has on the probability that a firm adjusts its employment or wages, or that it has fallen into arrears or expects to do so in the next six months. The orange brackets show the 95 percent confidence intervals around the point estimates.

decreasing wages, or both. For example, constrained firms were about 9 percentage points more likely to adjust labor costs without firing workers than unconstrained ones (37 versus 28 percent, respectively). The probability that FCFs reduced working hours or cut wages was, respectively, 21 and 15 percent, or 7.4 and 7.0 percentage points higher than firms that were not financially constrained. FCFs were also more likely to adjust along the extensive margin than unconstrained firms, displaying both a higher probability of firing workers (20 versus 16 percent) and a lower probability of hiring new workers (about 16 versus 21 percent). Lastly, FCFs were more likely to fall into arrears—a remarkable 22.7 percentage point increase over the probability of unconstrained firms in the likelihood of not being able to cover outstanding liabilities when facing liquidity problems.

While financial constraints affected the firms' ability to cope with the economic repercussions imposed by the pandemic, there were differences between constrained and unconstrained firms in terms of firm size (figure 6.5), but not firm age (figure 6.6). However, the differences across firm size varied significantly across the different margins of adjustment. For example, conditionally on being financially constrained, larger firms were less likely to cut hours and hire and fire workers, but were more likely to cut wages and be in arrears than smaller ones. The variance within these margins of adjustment across firms, however, was significantly greater for larger FCFs than for smaller FCFs, indicating that many of these differentials are not statistically significant. Regarding age, FCFs of all ages have been similarly impacted relative to unconstrained firms across most of the performance measures studied.[7] These findings highlight the potential distributional effects of shocks across firms, which, in turn, would affect aggregate outcomes such as productivity and growth.

**FIGURE 6.5  The Differential in Firm Performance between Financially Constrained and Unconstrained Firms Had Greater Variance for Large Firms than for Smaller Firms**

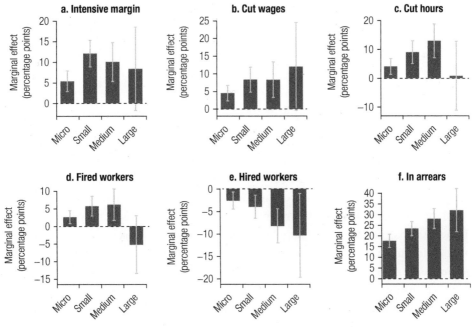

*Source:* Farazi and Lopez-Cordova 2023.

*Note:* The panels show the difference in the probability of each outcome (such as firing workers) between financially constrained and unconstrained firms across groupings by firm size. The estimates come from a linear probability model that controls for country, sector, severity of the shock brought on by the pandemic, and other firm-level characteristics. Firm size (micro, small, medium, and large) refers to the number of employees. The orange brackets show the 95 percent confidence intervals around the point estimates.

FIGURE 6.6 **There Was Little Difference in Firm Performance between Financially Constrained and Unconstrained Firms between Older and Younger Firms**

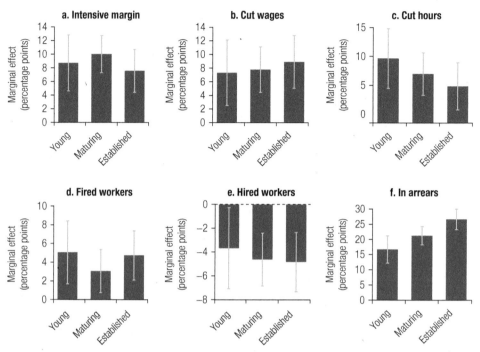

*Source:* Farazi and Lopez-Cordova 2023.

*Note:* The panels show the difference in the probability of each outcome (such as firing workers) between financially constrained and unconstrained firms across groupings by firm age. The estimates come from a linear probability model that controls for country, sector, the severity of shock brought on by the pandemic, and other firm-level characteristics. Firm age (young, maturing, and established) refers to years in operation. The orange brackets show the 95 percent confidence intervals around the point estimates.

## Government Support to Financially Constrained Firms

Policy makers around the world rapidly deployed a wide arsenal of tools to cope with the inevitable economic recession and mitigate the effects of the shock. Governments worldwide rolled out financial support schemes to help firms manage the pandemic shock while improving their odds of survival. The need for speedy and large support packages to ensure credit flow to firms, especially those facing liquidity constraints, was undisputable, especially at the onset of the COVID-19 pandemic and because the existing legal and regulatory infrastructure was ill-equipped to deal with an exogenous systemic shock like the pandemic. Attaining this goal meant not only refinancing measures to extend existing credit lines, but also extending new financing to existing and new clients given the increase in firms' financing needs.

Despite the unprecedented public rescue packages that governments in EMDEs and HICs alike mobilized to help affected firms during the pandemic, flaws in design and implementation made the support less effective than expected, as Cirera et al. (2021) show. Starkly, about 70 percent of the surveyed firms did not receive any form of government support after the onset of the pandemic (figure 6.7). Government interventions that helped address liquidity problems were the most common, although less than 5 percent of firms received them in the form of new loans. The bulk consisted of other liquidity support measures such as grants, payment deferrals, tax relief, or wage subsidies. About 25 percent of firms received such support. Business upgrading support measures, which in principle were not intended to address liquidity problems, benefited 13 percent of the firms.

Access to new loans varied widely across countries (figure 6.8). On the high end, the probability that a firm had access to new loans was about 14 percent in Chile and 10 percent in Tanzania and Türkiye; at the other extreme, access to new loans was basically not available for a large number of countries, including Nepal and Tajikistan (panel a). As in the earlier discussion, proxies for a country's level of financial development were positively correlated with the likelihood that firms received policy support in the form of new loans during the pandemic (panel b). That is, where domestic credit to the private sector or income per capita was higher (panel c), it was more likely that firms had access to new loans.

The question of how policy support to firms should be targeted became particularly salient during the COVID-19 pandemic, especially given the limited fiscal resources in many EMDEs. The risk of widespread firm closure as liquidity problems morphed into

**FIGURE 6.7  Only a Small Share of Firms Received Public Support during the COVID-19 Pandemic**

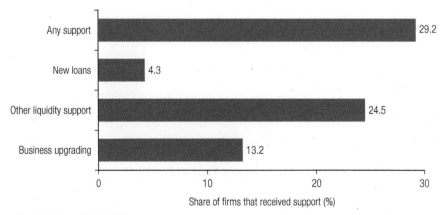

*Source:* Farazi and Lopez-Cordova 2023.

*Note:* The figure shows the unconditional mean that a firm in the sample received some form of public support in response to the pandemic. "Other liquidity support" refers to grants, payment deferrals, tax relief, or wage subsidies. "Business upgrading" considers technical assistance or subsidies for the adoption of digital technologies, health protocols, marketing, or improved managerial practices.

## FIGURE 6.8 The Probability of Getting a New Loan Varied Greatly during the COVID-19 Pandemic

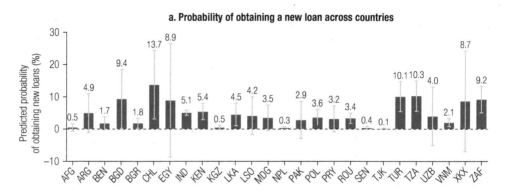

a. Probability of obtaining a new loan across countries

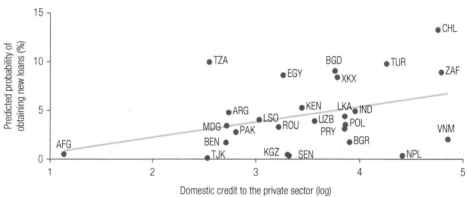

b. Greater access in countries with more developed financial systems

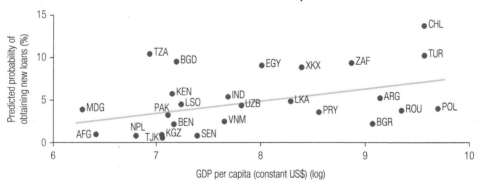

c. Greater access in more developed countries

*Source:* Farazi and Lopez-Cordova 2023.

*Note:* The figure shows probit estimates, controlling for size, sector, and severity of the shock brought on by the pandemic in a given country at the time of the survey. In panel a, the orange brackets show the 95 percent confidence intervals around the point estimates. The figure uses International Organization for Standardization country codes. GDP = gross domestic product.

insolvency ones—even for businesses with solid fundamentals before the pandemic—was of special concern for policy makers as this could leave profound scars and hamper prospects for long-term growth (Didier et al. 2021). Ideally, policy support should have been aimed at firms that were viable—that is, firms whose long-term profitability was positive—but were facing financial distress as a result of the pandemic shock (World Bank 2021). Unfortunately, ascertaining whether a firm was viable before the pandemic hit was very challenging. Moreover, the ability of governments to target support to firms, and the number of instruments available to do so, was severely limited in the first few months of the COVID-19 pandemic, when uncertainty was particularly high. This was especially so among countries with lower GDP per capita, whose administrative capabilities tend to be weaker.

The survey data explored in this chapter show that public support programs in EMDEs, aimed at mitigating firms' liquidity problems, were not as effective as expected in reaching financially constrained firms. Not only were larger firms more likely to receive support across all types of support measures, as suggested by Cirera et al. (2021), but financially constrained firms were less likely to have access to public support across firms of all size and age groups (figure 6.9). Importantly, the gap in access between financially constrained and unconstrained firms was the smallest with respect to access to new loans, which may be a sign that efforts at targeting new loans to the firms most in need might have been effective.

Regression estimates based on a linear probability model confirm these patterns. Specifically, FCFs displayed a propensity to have access to policy support that was about 3 to 5 percentage points lower than unconstrained firms, even after controlling for a host of firm characteristics and country and sector fixed effects. Overall, the results suggest that public support programs aimed at ameliorating liquidity problems may not have been effective in reaching one of the most vulnerable sets of firms.

## Access to Diversified Sources of Financing as a Risk Mitigation Strategy

The evidence around the COVID-19 pandemic highlights the importance of access to finance for firm performance when exogenous shocks hit developing economies. A large body of research complements the discussion in this chapter by exploring whether access to diversified sources of financing can help firms to weather shocks. Some argue that capital market financing can replace bank lending during banking crises, when capital markets thus act as a "spare tire" (Greenspan 1999). That is, well-developed stock and bond markets can mitigate the adverse effects of banking crises by providing an alternative source of financing when crises curtail the flow of bank credit to firms, thereby mitigating the effects of crises on firms. For example, Levine, Lin, and Xie (2016) show for a sample of listed firms that although economies do not necessarily use the spare tire during normal times, when banking crises hit, having the right legal

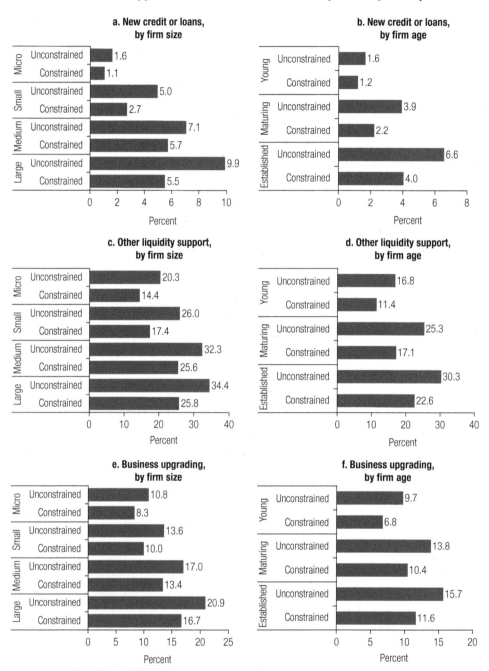

**FIGURE 6.9 Financially Constrained Firms Were Less Likely to Have Access to Public Support across Firms of All Size Groups and Age Groups**

**a. New credit or loans, by firm size**

Micro
- Unconstrained: 1.6
- Constrained: 1.1

Small
- Unconstrained: 5.0
- Constrained: 2.7

Medium
- Unconstrained: 7.1
- Constrained: 5.7

Large
- Unconstrained: 9.9
- Constrained: 5.5

Percent

**b. New credit or loans, by firm age**

Young
- Unconstrained: 1.6
- Constrained: 1.2

Maturing
- Unconstrained: 3.9
- Constrained: 2.2

Established
- Unconstrained: 6.6
- Constrained: 4.0

Percent

**c. Other liquidity support, by firm size**

Micro
- Unconstrained: 20.3
- Constrained: 14.4

Small
- Unconstrained: 26.0
- Constrained: 17.4

Medium
- Unconstrained: 32.3
- Constrained: 25.6

Large
- Unconstrained: 34.4
- Constrained: 25.8

Percent

**d. Other liquidity support, by firm age**

Young
- Unconstrained: 16.8
- Constrained: 11.4

Maturing
- Unconstrained: 25.3
- Constrained: 17.1

Established
- Unconstrained: 30.3
- Constrained: 22.6

Percent

**e. Business upgrading, by firm size**

Micro
- Unconstrained: 10.8
- Constrained: 8.3

Small
- Unconstrained: 13.6
- Constrained: 10.0

Medium
- Unconstrained: 17.0
- Constrained: 13.4

Large
- Unconstrained: 20.9
- Constrained: 16.7

Percent

**f. Business upgrading, by firm age**

Young
- Unconstrained: 9.7
- Constrained: 6.8

Maturing
- Unconstrained: 13.8
- Constrained: 10.4

Established
- Unconstrained: 15.7
- Constrained: 11.6

Percent

*Source:* Farazi and Lopez-Cordova 2023.

*Note:* This figure shows the fraction of firms that received public support in the aftermath of the pandemic shock. Firm size (micro, small, medium, and large) refers to the number of employees. Firm age (young, maturing, and established) refers to years in operation. In panels c and d, other liquidity support includes grants and deferral of taxes or other payments. In panels e and f, business upgrading includes digital technology, health protocols, marketing, and managerial practices.

infrastructure in place allows the stock market to mitigate the effects of the shock on firm performance and unemployment. Similarly, Amador and Nagengast (2016) provide evidence for a sample of firms in Portugal that adverse shocks to banks impair firm-level investments, particularly for small firms and those without access to alternative sources of finance.

Exogeneous adverse shocks may generate effects on both the demand for financing— the shock may increase uncertainty, leading firms to delay investments and financing— and the availability of funding due, for instance, to a contraction in the supply of bank debt. To disentangle these effects, Cortina, Didier, and Schmukler (2021) focus on public and private firms around the world with a revealed demand for credit, thereby exploring the effects of supply-side shocks. The analysis indicates that firms indeed tend to switch their sources of debt financing during banking crises. By increasing their borrowing in markets not directly hit by the shocks, firms compensate (partially and sometimes fully) for the decline in financing in shock-hit markets. The observed switches happened both between bond and syndicated loan financing as well as between domestic and international financing, depending on the source of the shock (at home or abroad).

Because debt markets typically carry different financing terms, these switches during banking crises were associated with significant effects not only on the amount borrowed, but also on debt maturity and currency composition. Firms that switched debt markets during crises maintained stable debt maturity at issuance, even though the maturity of newly issued debt tended to decline on average in individual debt markets. While the 2008–09 global financial crisis and domestic banking crises had similar effects on the maturity of debt issued, they triggered opposite effects on the currency composition of newly issued debt. In EMDEs, firms shifted toward domestic markets during the global financial crisis, and these firms issued more domestic currency debt. In contrast, during domestic banking crises, EMDE firms shifted to international markets issuing foreign currency debt.

Importantly, analysis shows that firms that moved across debt markets were on average substantially larger than firms that issued debt in only one market and did not change their financing composition.[8] Smaller firms exited the market or were constrained to certain debt markets. Moreover, banking crises prompted a change in the composition of firms using bonds and syndicated loan markets as a source of new financing. Relatively larger firms captured a larger share of the new debt issued during banking crises.

To the extent that smaller firms, especially private ones, are less likely to have access to multiple sources of financing (debt or equity) than larger firms, especially publicly listed ones, small firms are more prone to the effects of adverse supply-side shocks, such as those associated with a banking crisis. These results suggest that for smaller and younger firms in EMDEs, which are particularly dependent on debt as a source of finance, as shown in chapter 2, small fluctuations in the supply of bank finance would likely have significant impacts on their investments. These findings also raise the possibility that shocks to certain parts of the financial system would have differentiated impacts across firms.

## Conclusions

This chapter showed that financial constraints can constrain firms' ability to cope with adverse shocks. The COVID-19 pandemic presented a combination of demand and supply shocks that led to an abrupt and deep decline in firms' revenues, which in turn challenged their ability to cover operational costs and meet financial obligations and resulted in a cash crunch for many. New evidence presented in this chapter shows that during the COVID-19 pandemic, EMDE firms that had access to financing were better able to maintain employment levels and avoid falling into arrears. Nevertheless, many firms, particularly in countries with lower GDP per capita and less developed financial markets, were unable to mitigate the effects of the shock, partly because their access to financing was limited. Smaller private firms had the highest probability of being financially constrained during the COVID-19 pandemic. In contrast, younger firms had roughly similar probabilities of being financially constrained as more mature firms.

Access to diversified sources of financing could also help firms to weather shocks. This chapter discussed evidence showing that capital market financing can replace bank lending during banking crises, when capital markets might act as a "spare tire," allowing firms to lessen the adverse effects of the crisis on performance and unemployment. To the extent that smaller firms, especially private ones, are less likely to have access to multiple sources of financing (debt or equity) than larger firms (especially publicly listed ones), smaller firms are more prone to the effects of adverse supply-side shocks, such as those associated with a banking crisis. These results suggest that for smaller firms in EMDEs that are dependent on debt as a source of financing, small fluctuations in the supply of funds, such as financing from banks, can have sizable effects on their investments and, consequently, on productivity and growth. Hence, policy support should encompass a range of financial products (and financial providers) as dependence on a single source of financing can render firms vulnerable to shocks.[9]

The results in this chapter highlight that addressing financial constraints on smaller, viable private firms should be a critical element of the policy agenda to support firms in EMDEs. The results also highlight the importance of targeting in government programs to help firms to cope with shocks. Firms that were financially constrained after the pandemic began were overall less likely to have received public support, including access to new loans and other forms of liquidity support. These results stress the importance of refining the public sector's ability, in turbulent times, to target firm-level support toward businesses that are under financial stress and have limited access to finance, but that can remain viable in the long term. Shortcomings in targeted support effectively are a waste of precious public resources, reducing the effectiveness of public support. Chapter 7 provides a more in-depth discussion of the importance of targeting in supporting access to finance for smaller firms in EMDEs.

## Notes

1. For example, see studies of firms in Belgium (Degryse et al. 2019; Vermoesen, Deloof, and Laveren 2013), Italy (Cingano, Manaresi, and Sette 2016), the Netherlands (Zubair, Kabir, and Huang 2020), the United Kingdom (Akbar, Rehman, and Ormrod 2013), and the United States (Almeida et al. 2012; Duchin et al. 2022). Ayyagari, Demirgüç-Kunt, and Maksimovic (2021) analyze listed firms around the world, focusing on systemic sudden stop episodes.

2. Uncertainty indicators reached their highest values on record in reaction to the COVID-19 pandemic and its economic fallout (Ahir, Bloom, and Furceri 2022; Altig et al. 2020).

3. See, for example, Apedo-Amah et al. (2020); Baqaee and Farhi (2020); Eichenbaum, Rebelo, and Trabandt (2020); and Guerrieri et al. (2020).

4. The surveys have been implemented in waves, with wave 1 undertaken at the early stages of the pandemic and lockdowns, from April to October 2020. Wave 2 was undertaken between November 2020 and April 2021. Wave 3 is underway in several EMDEs. The questionnaires used across waves are broadly similar, with minor differences associated with the addition of new questions or changes in the wording of some, based on lessons learned from previous waves and feedback from stakeholders. The BPS database spans more than 50 countries and covers more than 100,0000 MSMEs and large enterprises in all the main sectors of the economy (agriculture, manufacturing, retail, and other services, including construction). Data from waves 2 and 3 were used for the purposes of this volume because they contained more detailed information on indicators of financial stress.

5. For more details on how to map these definitions to specific question in the BPS, see Farazi and Lopez-Cordova (2023).

6. However, when a more stringent definition of FCFs was used that considered a drop in sales greater than or equal to 70 percent, women-led firms were more likely to be financially constrained, and the result was statistically significant.

7. The only notable result is that young firms (age 4 years or younger) were estimated to be more likely to fire workers when faced with liquidity problems than young unconstrained firms, and this differential was larger than for more mature firms.

8. These findings are consistent with those of Demirgüç-Kunt, Martinez Peria, and Tressel (2020), suggesting that large, publicly listed firms reduced their leverage less than private firms in the aftermath of the global financial crisis.

9. There is indeed a range of debt products that can help small and medium enterprises overcome their limited credit history and/or limited ability to pledge collateral—such as asset-based lending, supply chain financing, and cash flow lending, to name a few.

## References

Ahir, H., N. Bloom, and D. Furceri. 2022. "The World Uncertainty Index." Working Paper 29763, National Bureau of Economic Research, Cambridge, MA.

Akbar, S., S. Rehman, and P. Ormrod. 2013. "The Impact of Recent Financial Shocks on the Financing and Investment Policies of UK Private Firms." *International Review of Financial Analysis* 26: 59–70.

Almeida, H., M. Campello, B. Laranjeira, and S. Weisbenner. 2012. "Corporate Debt Maturity and the Real Effects of the 2007 Credit Crisis." *Critical Finance Review* 1 (1): 3–58.

Altig, D., S. R. Baker, J. M. Barrero, N. Bloom, P. Bunn, S. Chen, S. J. Davis, J. Leather, B. H. Meyer, E. Mihaylov, P. Mizen, N. B. Parker, T. Renault, P. Smietanka, and G. Thwaites. 2020. "Economic Uncertainty before and during the COVID-19 Pandemic." NBER Working Paper 27418, National Bureau of Economic Research, Cambridge, MA.

Amador, J., and A. Nagengast. 2016. "The Effect of Bank Shocks on Firm-Level and Aggregate Investment." Working Paper 1914, European Central Bank, Frankfurt.

Apedo-Amah, M. C., B. Avdiu, X. Cirera, M. Cruz, E. Davies, A. Grover, L. Iacovone, U. Kilinc, D. Medvedev, F. O. Maduko, S. Poupakis, J. Torres, and T. T. Tran. 2020. "Unmasking the Impact of COVID-19 on Businesses: Firm Level Evidence from across the World." Policy Research Working Paper 9434, World Bank, Washington, DC.

Ayyagari, M., A. Demirgüç-Kunt, and V. Maksimovic. 2021. "How Common Are Credit-Less Recoveries? Firm-Level Evidence on the Role of Financial Markets in Crisis Recovery." *Journal of Corporate Finance* 69: 102016.

Baqaee, D., and E. Farhi. 2020. "Nonlinear Production Networks with an Application to the COVID-19 Crisis." NBER Working Paper 27281, National Bureau of Economic Research, Cambridge, MA.

Chen, S., and D. Lee. 2020. "Small and Vulnerable: Small Firm Productivity in the Great Productivity Slowdown." IMF Working Paper WP/20/294, International Monetary Fund, Washington, DC.

Chodorow-Reich, G. 2014. "The Employment Effects of Credit Market Disruptions: Firm-Level Evidence from the 2008-9 Financial Crisis." *Quarterly Journal of Economics* 26 (1): 1–59.

Cingano, F., F. Manaresi, and E. Sette. 2016. "Does Credit Crunch Investment Down? New Evidence on the Real Effects of the Bank-Lending Channel." *Review of Financial Studies* 29 (10): 2737–73.

Cirera, X., M. Cruz, E. Davies, A. Grover, L. Iacovone, J. E. Lopez Cordova, D. Medvedev, F. Okechukwu Maduko, G. Nayyar, S. Reyes Ortega, and J. Torres. 2021. "Policies to Support Businesses through the COVID-19 Shock: A Firm-Level Perspective." Policy Research Working Paper 9506, World Bank, Washington, DC.

Cortina, J. J., T. Didier, and S. Schmukler. 2021. "Global Corporate Debt during Crises: Implications of Switching Borrowing across Markets." *Journal of International Economics* 131: 103487.

Degryse, H., O. De Jonghe, S. Jakovljević, K. Mulier, and G. Schepens. 2019. "Identifying Credit Supply Shocks with Bank-Firm Data: Methods and Applications." *Journal of Financial Intermediation* 40: 100813.

Demirgüç-Kunt, A., M. S. Martinez Peria, and T. Tressel. 2020. "The Global Financial Crisis and the Capital Structure of Firms: Was the Impact More Severe among SMEs and Non-Listed Firms?" *Journal of Corporate Finance* 60: 101514.

Didier, T., F. Huneeus, M. Larrain, and S. L. Schmukler. 2021. "Financing Firms in Hibernation during the COVID-19 Pandemic." *Journal of Financial Stability* 53: 100837.

Duchin, R., X. Martin, R. Michaely, and I. Wang. 2022. "Concierge Treatment from Banks: Evidence from the Paycheck Protection Program." *Journal of Corporate Finance* 72: 102124.

Eichenbaum, M., S. Rebelo, and M. Trabandt. 2020. "The Macroeconomics of Epidemics." NBER Working Paper 26882, National Bureau of Economic Research, Cambridge, MA.

Farazi, S., and J. E. Lopez-Cordova. 2023. "Financial Constraints, Firm Performance, and Policy Support during the COVID-19 Pandemic." Background paper for this volume. World Bank, Washington, DC.

Granja, J., and S. Moreira. 2023. "Product Innovation and Credit Market Disruptions." *Review of Financial Studies* 36 (5): 1930–69.

Greenspan, A. 1999. "Do Efficient Financial Markets Mitigate Financial Crises?" Financial Markets Conference of the Federal Reserve Bank of Atlanta.

Guerrieri, V., G. Lorenzoni, L. Straub, and I. Werning. 2020. "Macroeconomic Implications of COVID-19: Can Negative Supply Shocks Cause Demand Shortages?" NBER Working Paper 26918, National Bureau of Economic Research, Cambridge, MA.

Huber, K. 2018. "Disentangling the Effects of a Banking Crisis: Evidence from German Firms and Counties." *American Economic Review* 108 (3): 868–98.

Levine, R., C. Lin, and W. Xie. 2016. "Spare Tire? Stock Markets, Banking Crises, and Economic Recoveries." *Journal of Financial Economics* 120 (1): 81–101.

Siemer, M. 2019. "Employment Effects of Financial Constraints during the Great Recession." *Review of Economics and Statistics* 101 (1): 16–29.

Vermoesen, V., M. Deloof, and E. Laveren. 2013. "Long-Term Debt Maturity and Financing Constraints of SMEs during the Global Financial Crisis." *Small Business Economics* 41: 433–48.

World Bank. 2021. "Supporting Firms in Restructuring and Recovery." World Bank, Washington, DC.

Zubair, S., R. Kabir, and X. Huang. 2020. "Does the Financial Crisis Change the Effect of Financing on Investment? Evidence from Private SMEs." *Journal of Business Research* 110: 456–63.

# 7. Implications for Policy Action

## Introduction

This volume has shown that there are acute financial constraints on private firms in middle-income countries (MICs) and these constraints have a sizable negative impact on aggregate outcomes, such as productivity and growth. Drawing from a newly constructed data set of 2.5 million private firms across MICs and high-income countries (HICs), the volume has shown that financial market inefficiencies—namely, financial frictions and market failures—constrain financial flows to firms and, consequently, negatively affect individual firm performance (the *within* margin) and the allocation of resources across firms (the *between* margin). On the latter, the estimates presented in chapter 5 showed that mitigating these inefficiencies, thereby relaxing firms' financial constraints, can lead to aggregate productivity gains of up to 86 percent in MICs, with the largest gains observed among MICs with lower gross domestic product (GDP) per capita. These gains stem from a reallocation of financial resources toward financially constrained yet productive firms.

The misallocation of finance is particularly detrimental to smaller firms in a country. The estimation results in chapter 5 showed that larger productivity gains would accrue for smaller firms than for larger firms from a reallocation of financial resources toward financially constrained yet productive firms. That is, smaller firms would benefit the most from a more efficient allocation of capital across firms. The results in chapter 4 also showed that smaller firms tend to experience a larger boost in growth and productive capabilities with capital market financing. For example, in the year of capital raising issuance of equity or bonds, the growth rate of total assets for the smallest firms in the sample is on average 37 percentage points higher than that for firms of similar size that did not raise capital. In contrast, the differential for the largest firms in the sample is only about 7 percentage points. These findings indicate that firms are not using the new funds just to change their capital structure or increase financial investments; rather, with relaxed financial constraints, firms can better realize expected growth opportunities.

In MICs, the smallest private firms, particularly those with fewer than 100 employees, face the largest financing gaps. The results in chapter 2 showed that the debt financing gap is larger for the smaller firms. Although there is virtually no variation in leverage ratios across firms of different sizes in HICs, smaller private firms tend to have significantly lower debt-to-assets ratios than larger firms in MICs.

For example, on average, the smallest private firms in the sample have debt-to-assets ratios of around 65 percent in HICs, whereas similarly sized firms in MICs have leverage ratios averaging 40 percent. The smallest private firms in MICs have even lower leverage ratios, around 20 percent. The differential among similarly sized firms between MICs and HICs declines as firms grow, with virtually no differences observed for the largest private firms and publicly listed firms. These results thus quantify the so-called "small and medium enterprise (SME) financing gap," which has been an elusive feature in discussions of firms' access to finance. Overall, the results showed that firms' capital structure varies significantly along the firm size distribution for private firms in MICs.

Smaller, innovative private firms in MICs make limited use of both debt and external equity financing. For example, the estimations in chapter 3 showed that small firms with high levels of research and development (R&D) have on average lower leverage ratios than small, low R&D firms or large firms. The differential in leverage is larger in MICs than in HICs, especially among the smallest firms, indicating that access to debt financing is more challenging for those smaller, innovative firms in MICs. Furthermore, the significant underdevelopment of private markets for equity financing in emerging market and developing economies (EMDEs) constrains the availability of equity financing, leaving smaller, innovative firms underserved. The results also showed that the bulk of venture capital (VC) and private equity (PE) investments in MICs is concentrated in relatively larger firms. For example, private firms with more than 350 employees accounted for roughly 70 percent of the VC investments in MICs during 2010–19, compared to 35 percent in HICs.

The evidence emerging from the COVID-19 pandemic discussed in chapter 6 reinforced these results. Smaller private firms in EMDEs had the highest probability of being financially constrained during the pandemic. Firms with 100 or more workers had an 11 percent probability of being financially constrained, whereas for firms with fewer than 20 workers, the probability jumped to more than 20 percent. Nonetheless, financially constrained firms were less prevalent in countries where domestic credit to the private sector and gross domestic product per capita were higher.

Furthermore, financial constraints not only hinder the productivity and growth of firms, but also constrain their ability to cope with adverse shocks. For instance, the COVID-19 pandemic was an exogenous shock that led to an abrupt, steep decline in firms' revenues, which in turn challenged their ability to cover expenses and meet their financial obligations. The results in chapter 6 for a sample of firms in EMDEs showed that during the pandemic, firms that had access to financing were better able to maintain employment levels and avoid falling into arrears. Many firms, particularly in countries with lower GDP per capita and less developed financial markets, were unable to mitigate the effects of the shock, partly because their access to external sources of financing was limited.

Access to diversified sources of financing can also help firms to weather shocks. The evidence in chapter 4 showed that capital market financing can replace bank lending during banking crises, when capital markets might act as a "spare tire," allowing firms to lessen the adverse effects of the crisis on performance and employment. Hence, firms with limited access to multiple sources of financing (whether debt or equity) are more exposed to the effects of negative shocks, such as those associated with a banking crisis. Larger firms are typically better able to cope with such shocks, especially publicly listed firms with access to capital markets. In contrast, for smaller firms in MICs, which are often dependent on banks for external finance, small fluctuations in bank credit can have sizable effects on their investments and growth.

Overall, the analyses in this volume pointed to size-related inefficiencies in financial markets for EMDEs, which render smaller firms more financially constrained than larger firms and firms of comparable size in HICs. Addressing the financial constraints on smaller private firms should thus be a critical element of the policy agenda to support firms in EMDEs. Financial sector policies need to address the key financial market failures and frictions underlying the challenges in access to finance for SMEs. The following are at the core of these financial constraints: (1) the greater opacity of SMEs (for example, SMEs tend to lack reliable financial statements); (2) their relatively high riskiness (partly a reflection of lower capabilities); and (3) their lack of assets that can be used as collateral, which could mitigate the challenges associated with (1) and (2). Thus, compared to larger firms, investors and creditors have greater difficulty in assessing smaller private firms' prospects and creditworthiness, monitoring their actions, and enforcing contractual obligations—all of which contribute to a lower likelihood of extending financing to these smaller firms. These challenges tend to be particularly marked in countries with less developed financial systems as additional challenges emerge from inefficiencies in the financial sector itself that also have a disproportionately higher impact on smaller firms in the country. For example, the relatively high transaction costs of processing relatively small loans and inadequate lending technologies can hinder outreach to SMEs. A key recent development has been the emergence and increased adoption of new financial technologies, the so-called fintech. Fintech solutions address some of the key financial market failures and frictions underlying the challenges in access to finance for SMEs. Box 7.1 discusses how fintech may be mitigating these challenges. Furthermore, missing markets are a critical challenge in many EMDEs.

The evidence in the volume supports the active engagement of policy makers in addressing size-induced financial market inefficiencies and unlocking the constraints on SME financing to boost productivity and growth, but how to do so? The rest of this chapter discusses the policy recommendations that emerge from the analyses in this volume. Policy makers should take an all-encompassing approach that: (1) fosters the enabling and supportive environment for debt and equity financing, and (2) considers more targeted approaches to improve access where financing gaps are most severe. Although nontargeted interventions benefit all firms, they tend to benefit the smaller firms in a country disproportionately. In the context of this volume, targeted

## Can Fintech Help Close the Gaps in Firm Financing?

Although they were not directly explored in this volume, the more widespread adoption of financial technology (fintech) solutions may be changing the landscape for firm financing, especially debt financing for small and medium enterprises (SMEs).[a] For instance, the use of big data and fintech can mitigate frictions related to information asymmetries by enhancing access to alternative sources of data. Instead of relying on a firm's credit history or collateral to fill information gaps about its ability to repay its debt, lenders can use data-driven credit scores or access real-time payment data to extend credit to previously underserved firms (such as SMEs). For example, embedded finance providers, ranging from e-commerce and logistics platforms to consumer goods distribution networks, are able to leverage transactional data on orders, inventory, sales, or receivables to provide working capital financing for firms. This allows firms to leverage their broader business relationships to provide alternative recourses to lenders when the firms lack collateral for debt financing. Moreover, lenders can reach firms at lower costs through digital channels. By facilitating access to finance through "branchless banking," fintech solutions can improve the outreach to smaller firms in more remote areas, thereby reducing the typically high transaction costs associated with servicing these firms through conventional bank branches. Fintech solutions also have the potential to mitigate the high transaction costs of small-transaction finance and concerns about scalability in SME financing, by increasing digitalization, automation, and adoption of artificial intelligence.

However, fintech solutions are not a panacea. Fintech solutions do not tackle all the constraints on access to finance for underserved firms, and they raise new obstacles that, in many instances, can be constraining, especially in the context of emerging market and developing economies (EMDEs). For example, crowdfunding could suffer from free-riding problems and high monitoring costs due to the large number of investors and entrepreneurs competing for funding (Guenther, Johan, and Schweizer 2018). Agency problems can also arise in crowdfunding: reward-based crowdfunding involves risks tied to product development and delivery, whereas equity-based crowdfunding and peer-to-peer crowdlending involve conflicts between shareholders and debtholders, which can lead to underinvestment and risk shifting, among other forms of moral hazard (Cumming and Johan 2019; Farag and Johan 2021; Strausz 2017). Digital financial services also increase the potential risks associated with data privacy and consumer and investor protection. Thus, these services may require new regulatory frameworks and financial infrastructure—such as systems for digital identification and authentication, legal and regulatory frameworks for data protection and data privacy that adequately address cybersecurity risks, and regulatory frameworks that enable the use of electronic assets for trading or collateral, among others. Furthermore, challenges associated with the use of alternative data and automated approaches for credit risk assessments could introduce distortions into lending decisions. For example, there is the potential for discrimination biases (such as gender, race, and geographical location) that arguably have a larger impact on underserved segments.[b] The opacity of the algorithms makes it particularly difficult to address these biases, thus complicating the adoption of safeguards. In EMDEs, where the enabling environment for firm financing is often underdeveloped, these new challenges associated with digital financing for firms could further hinder access. This is ultimately an empirical question left for future research.

a. Although expanding, the use of fintech remains relatively limited for the financing of firms in most EMDEs, especially when contrasted to high-income countries. See Didier et al. (2022); and CCAF, World Bank, and World Economic Forum (2022).
b. According to Bartlett et al. (2022), the nature of discrimination may change from human biases to statistical discrimination through the widespread use of big data.

interventions focus exclusively on SMEs or a subset of them. Although the volume did not delve deeply into the underlying types of financial frictions and market failures constraining SME finance, these inefficiencies are markedly different for debt and equity financing. Hence, the discussion emphasizes the importance of a differentiated approach in supporting debt and equity financing for firms.

## Policy Support Needs to Take a Differentiated Approach toward Debt and Equity Financing

Financial sector policies aimed at closing the financing gaps for firms in EMDEs must focus on supporting widespread and efficient access to debt financing for SMEs. The estimates in chapter 5 showed that about 65–85 percent of the misallocation of finance across firms stems from a scale effect—an inefficient allocation of the total amount of finance to firms—rather than a composition effect. The results showed that removing financial market inefficiencies to relax the overall level of firms' financial constraints, while keeping the debt-equity composition unchanged, could lead to aggregate productivity gains of up to 73 percent in MICs. In practice, debt constitutes the largest and most important source of finance for a vast majority of private firms in the developing world. Hence, the core focus of policy initiatives aimed at fostering financing for SMEs should be on debt financing.

Although in practice debt is a crucial source of financing for SMEs, equity financing can be powerful in promoting innovation. Debt and equity financing play important but distinct roles in supporting firms' productivity and growth. Equity financing is a more effective way of funding firms with innovative activities. These activities are inherently risky and generally entail investments in intangible assets that provide limited collateral value. Investments in intangible assets could thus be hard to finance with debt, especially when firms lack other sources of collateral. The results in chapter 4 suggested that this is indeed the case for firms in EMDEs. Equity but not bond financing is associated with rapid expansion of the productive capabilities of firms with high levels of R&D expenditures, especially in terms of intangible assets. A key implication of this result is that limited access to equity financing can hinder investments in intangibles and distort firms' investment decisions—for instance, toward safer and liquid but potentially less profitable and less innovative projects—thereby constraining their productivity and growth.

The underdevelopment of equity markets in EMDEs constrains the undertaking of innovative activities, impacting aggregate productivity and growth. The results in chapter 3 showed that VC financing is skewed toward a narrow set of high-tech sectors, such as the software industry, whereas PE investments tend to focus on more traditional sectors. These investment patterns suggest that private markets for equity financing have played a limited role in advancing substantial technological change in EMDEs. Indeed, the estimations in chapter 5 showed that countries with more knowledge- and technology-related outputs, and thus arguably a larger share of firms engaging in innovative activities, would benefit the most from improvement in the allocation of capital between debt and equity. Countries with more innovative activities could obtain sizable productivity gains from rebalancing the composition of financing to firms and improving their access to equity finance. These results reinforce the idea that firms' capital structure matters for aggregate productivity, at least in part because of the value of equity financing for innovative firms.

With a holistic approach, policy can be effective in developing equity markets. A well-rounded approach to developing the overall landscape for equity financing and entrepreneurship and innovation would improve the likelihood of successful interventions. The experience of HICs indicates that supporting equity market development is a costly endeavor, often with long lead times, and it requires a long-term commitment to reach sustained impact. Moreover, policy makers need to think of equity market development across its full spectrum—from seed and angel investors to venture capitalists and private and public markets. Individual segments should not be viewed and supported in isolation, as they would typically have upstream and downstream linkages—for example, earlier market stages can support deal flows to later stages, and analogously, the later stages can be exit options for earlier investors. In addition, the design of government programs to support private equity market development is particularly important, as these plans can affect the program effectiveness.[1] In EMDEs, these difficulties can be even more pronounced as fostering the development of equity markets entails tackling a complex set of interrelated demand- and supply-side challenges. For example, the evidence in chapter 3 pointed toward deficiencies in the entrepreneurial environment as well as in the broader enabling environment for equity financing and the lack of domestic risk capital, which are reflected in the underdevelopment of the full spectrum of equity markets, including public markets.

Policy makers must also be cognizant of the trade-offs in allocating resources to support equity financing versus debt financing, especially when fiscal resources are scarce. There is limited empirical evidence that would help to focus discussions on how debt and equity financing might compete with and/or complement each other as sources of financing for firms in EMDEs. The evidence in this volume highlights a few important considerations. The foremost consideration is that policy makers need to be realistic about both the desirability of policy interventions as well as their feasibility and impact. Carvajal and Didier (2024) highlight that the feasibility and impact of policy support programs depend on individual country contexts. A consideration in this regard is the outreach of different markets. Debt financing is the most important source of financing for firms, and support programs for debt financing can have widespread reach. In contrast, programs supporting equity financing typically have limited reach, covering a small set of firms, often in a narrow set of industries. That is the case even in HICs. For example, Lerner and Nanda (2020) point out that firms backed by VC comprise less than 0.5 percent of the firms that are born each year in the United States. In other words, equity financing is a viable funding option for a few firms, suggesting that, at least in the near term, debt financing will continue to be the key financing source for SMEs, including innovative firms.

The results also suggest that policy interventions to support equity market development are more likely to succeed when certain preconditions are in place, such as the availability of risky capital, the existence of a strong institutional investor base, the development of various segments providing equity financing for firms, and the degree of development of the entrepreneurial environment. These conditions are more likely to be observed among the more financially developed MICs, raising questions about the effectiveness of interventions in EMDEs more broadly. However, empirical evidence remains scarce. The targeting of policies is another critical aspect to ensure the effectiveness and impact of policy support on productivity and growth.

Research on the effectiveness of specific government policies supporting the financing of innovation and the development of equity markets, especially private markets, remains scarce. For instance, there has been no systematic evaluation of the costs of government intervention in supporting private market development, even in more developed MICs. There has also been limited evidence on the shape that government interventions should take—for example, the most effective form of ownership structure for government sponsored VC funds. At the core of this lack of research is the lack of data. Although information is typically available for entrepreneurs who have obtained (private and public) equity financing with or without government support, information on the counterfactual, that is, those who did not get equity financing, is often missing. More research is needed in this area, especially on the effectiveness of interactions among different government policies, such as between initiatives supporting the development of private markets for equity financing and those fostering entrepreneurial activities.

## Policy Targeting Should Reflect the Larger Financing Gaps for Smaller and Innovative Firms

The findings in this volume indicate that in supporting debt financing, there is a role for financial sector policies that target firms based on their size, which is an effective proxy for financial constraints in EMDEs. For example, the evidence emerging from the years of the COVID-19 pandemic discussed in chapter 6 highlighted the importance of targeting in government programs to help firms to cope with shocks. Although ex ante targeting the set of financially constrained firms was a complex task when the pandemic hit, ex post evidence indicates that firm size would have constituted an adequate targeting parameter. This is consistent with other analyses in this volume that show that the smaller firms in a country tend to be more financially constrained than larger ones. Although the size of a firm is a proxy for its financial constraints, the age of the firm is not. For example, the results in chapter 6 showed that younger firms had roughly similar probabilities of being financially constrained as more mature firms during the pandemic, suggesting that younger firms were not particularly vulnerable to shocks. In addition, chapter 5 showed that relaxing financial constraints based on firm age did not unequivocally yield positive productivity gains in all countries in the sample, thus casting doubt on using firm age as a relevant proxy for policy action. The importance of access to finance for firms at the beginning of their life cycle is a topic that deserves more research.

Size-based targeting in financial sector policies should not translate into unconditional support to firms simply based on their size. The viability of firms is a critical aspect for policy targeting, for instance, to avoid supporting the proliferation of zombie firms.[2] Policies should balance the need for access to finance with the need for financial discipline and accountability. Policies deployed through financial institutions can provide incentives for lenders to do business as usual through their due diligence processes, assessing firms' prospects and their capacity to repay in the case of credit providers, and thereby ensuring that capital flows to firms with better prospects. Nonetheless, there could be perverse incentives for both firms and financial institutions, which puts a premium on policy design. For example, targeted policies should be carefully designed to avoid creating policy-induced thresholds that distort firms' incentives to grow. Banks may have incentives to push loans to certain segments or regions to meet quotas or lending targets set by the government, which can lead to overlending and high default rates as the loans may not be sustainable or viable for borrowers.

Targeted financial sector interventions should aim at addressing the key financial market failures and frictions underlying the challenges in access to finance for SMEs. They often focus on reducing the perceived and real risks associated with debt financing for smaller private firms. One of the core size-induced market failures for debt financing is related to information asymmetries, which tend to increase the (often high) risks of engaging with smaller firms as lenders are unable to assess their financial viability. In the context of limited information, the lack of assets that can effectively serve as collateral and the limited scalability of lending technologies for smaller firms may further amplify these risks. Hence, targeted interventions aimed at mitigating financial market inefficiencies preventing viable SMEs from accessing financing should intentionally focus on: (1) improving information on SMEs; (2) "de-risking" SMEs, including scaling up financing to the segment to foster risk diversification; and (3) creating missing markets. Examples of such policies include partial credit guarantees, lines of credit, and co-investments. The relative importance of these different markets depends critically on country context.

The direct engagement of private capital in a sustainable manner is critical for the development of firm financing in EMDEs. Policy makers should thus place significant emphasis on improving additionality and crowding in private capital, while minimizing distortions and outright avoiding crowding out effects, when designing targeted policies. Clear graduation criteria are also crucial for the sustainability and effectiveness of targeted policies. For firms, including SMEs, graduation would entail ensuring that policies aim at a transition toward market-based financing; for financial institutions, it would entail a transition toward commercially viable engagement with the targeted segment, such as SMEs.

Although policy targeting is complex, it is imperative for equity financing, due in large part to the scarcity of this financing source in EMDEs. The lack of a diverse set of options for financing can increase the attractiveness of equity financing for firms seeking to diversify their funding sources. Even though equity can fund any type of investment, it generally disproportionately benefits firms with investments in intangible assets, such as small, high-tech, and/or high R&D firms, which often have difficulties in accessing debt financing. Hence, the equity financing gap is most acute for smaller private firms undertaking innovative activities in EMDEs. However, equity is an expensive source of financing compared to debt, and entrepreneurs may be reluctant to accept external shareholders, regardless of economic or financial considerations. Furthermore, many start-ups and SMEs are not investment ready—they might not understand what equity investors are looking for or how to "sell" their businesses to potential investors. These weaknesses, in turn, can compromise the effectiveness of supply-side interventions, such as initiatives to develop equity markets. While public sector support can be particularly important in the early-stage segments of equity markets, thus addressing the scarcity of funding for smaller firms, the targeting of programs for equity financing should go beyond a size-based approach. That is, the policy agenda must recognize that for a subset of SMEs—notably, innovative ones—a more balanced approach between access to debt and equity financing would be valuable.[3]

## A Supportive Enabling Environment Is the Backbone of Firm Financing

Financial sector regulators can contribute to improved access to finance for firms by promoting a favorable legal and regulatory environment. Such an environment establishes the rules within which all the financial institutions, financial instruments, and financial markets operate in a given country. Legal and regulatory frameworks are complemented by sound financial infrastructure that improves the efficiency and effectiveness of financial intermediation. For example, deficiencies in credit information systems, secure transaction frameworks, and insolvency regimes can hinder the efficient functioning of financial systems, even in the presence of an otherwise flawless legal and regulatory framework. It is worth noting upfront that reforms to the enabling environment can take years to develop. Changes in laws and regulations are often just the initial steps in effectively supporting and improving the landscape for firm financing. Effective implementation, including enforcement, is critical.

These nontargeted interventions do not focus specifically on a subset of private firms, such as SMEs, but they tend to entail disproportionate benefits for this set of firms. Fostering the enabling environment for debt and equity financing complements more directed interventions. Moreover, Carvajal and Didier (2024) emphasize that the policy agenda to complete the enabling environment supporting firm financing carries very limited fiscal costs, while the benefits could be sizable, especially for SMEs.

This is the case for policies aimed at strengthening the financial infrastructure, which typically reduce the information asymmetries and legal uncertainties that increase the risks of SME financing for lenders and investors. Because the challenges of opacity of information and high investment riskiness are more severe for the smaller firms in a country, they would benefit the most from such interventions. For example, strengthening credit information systems to expand the coverage and depth of information—for example, by including alternative data such as payment transactions, as well as positive and negative data—would facilitate the flow of information, thereby mitigating information asymmetries and reducing the adverse selection and moral hazard concerns that are typical in SME financing. In effect, the need for physical collateral could be replaced by, or at least supplemented with, reputational collateral. Moreover, increased access to reliable information could facilitate the adoption of automated screening methods, such as credit scoring models, which would help to address the high transaction costs of lending to SMEs, for example.[4] Similarly, effective collateral systems can reduce the risks and losses for lenders. For example, developing secured transaction frameworks that enable the use of movable assets as collateral can foster access to finance for small firms by addressing collateral mismatch between borrowers and lenders. For these firms, movable assets typically account for a large share of their assets.[5]

The findings in chapter 5 also highlighted the importance of effective insolvency systems. These would ensure the existence of robust exit mechanisms to minimize the prevalence of zombie firms, thereby reducing the amounts of capital and labor sunk into these firms and facilitating asset reallocation when firms become unproductive.[6] Insolvency laws are critical for creating a level playing field that permits nonviable businesses to exit swiftly and predictably, thereby permitting viable businesses to restructure when needed and playing a pivotal role in saving jobs. For example, the estimations in chapter 5 showed that deficiencies in insolvency systems can distort incentives—for example, by supporting inefficient loan evergreening—that increase the likelihood and prolong the survival of zombie firms. Moreover, the findings showed that weak insolvency systems lock up not only capital, but also labor in low productivity uses. To the extent that labor released from exiting firms is absorbed by more productive firms, there could be gains in aggregate output.

Supporting the enabling environment for a wide range of debt financing options could also help to address the marked financing gaps faced by some firms, including innovative SMEs. Supporting access to finance for SMEs should not be focused on bank loans alone; it can be achieved through a range of financial products (and financial providers). Various debt products can help SMEs to overcome their limited credit history and/or limited ability to pledge collateral—such as asset-based lending, supply chain financing, and cash flow lending. For example, factoring can be an important source of working capital financing for SMEs, whereas leasing can be valuable for investment finance. Policy makers should thus support the legal and regulatory frameworks for this wider set of debt financing products. Access to diversified sources of financing could also help firms to weather shocks. For instance, alternative financing sources might act as a "spare tire" in times of crisis in the banking sector, allowing firms to mitigate the effects of a crisis on their performance. Furthermore, the development of these markets can be important for firms undertaking innovative activities and/or investing in intangible assets as many of these firms have limited tangible assets to offer as collateral for bank financing. Policy makers could also foster the use of intangible assets as collateral in debt financing, as the evidence points to significant challenges in this area.[7] However, there is limited evidence on the effectiveness of specific policies supporting intangible collateralization in the context of EMDEs, which calls for more research on this topic.

## Improving the Availability of and Access to Data

Policy makers need to consider the unique circumstances of each country and prioritize evidence-based policies that address the challenges of the SME financing gap. Therefore, the recommendations put forward in this chapter are cautious, without being excessively prescriptive, on how to support debt and equity financing. A rigorous, data-driven assessment of the key constraints on firm financing and their underlying causes within the context of individual countries is important not only for the design of policies, but also for policy implementation, including the prioritization and sequencing of an appropriate set of public policy interventions. A data-driven assessment can also enhance the effectiveness of interventions by enabling the implementation of effective monitoring and evaluation frameworks. Analysis of firm financing based on high-quality, granular data can help to enhance the effectiveness of targeted support policies, for example, by allowing an assessment of policy additionality.

However, there is a generalized lack of data on firm financing, especially on the various sources of debt and equity financing for private firms across the developing world. There is a major gap in standardized, accurate, granular, and frequent data on firm financing, especially for SMEs. The scope of the empirical analyses in this volume was largely constrained by the availability of firm-level data. For instance, certain chapters focused on a selected set of MICs, instead of a wider sample of low- and middle-income countries, solely because of data availability. Despite these significant data limitations, this volume presented novel results on several long-standing, policy-relevant challenges related to financing gaps for firms in EMDEs. For instance, the analyses in this volume shed light on the extent to which inefficiencies in financial markets constrain private firms and how they may vary across firms of different sizes and ages; the impact of financial constraints on the allocation of resources across firms and on allowing existing firms to expand, improve, and cope with shocks; and the relevance of the composition of financing sources—namely, debt versus equity—for firms' productivity and growth; among others.[8] Overall, the data gap is especially marked in countries where data are most needed, such as those with less developed financial systems, where financial inefficiencies can be more constraining. Importantly, access to data supports not only the decision-making processes of policy makers (including central banks, regulators, and development institutions), but also those of financial institutions and the private sector at large.

Therefore, improving the availability of and access to data is crucial toward an effective policy agenda. Policy makers should prioritize the collection of and access to more granular and better quality data on firm financing and performance to foster evidence-based policies to tackle the challenges of the SME financing gap. Although several EMDEs have taken important actions to expand their statistical base, stepping-up efforts are still needed to develop and improve the national building blocks for effective and comprehensive data collection, including by using regular firm-level surveys.

## Conclusions

Overall, the various analyses in this volume point to size-related inefficiencies in financial markets in EMDEs that render smaller firms more financially constrained than larger firms. The results show that relaxing these financial constraints on smaller firms—for instance, through policy action that mitigates these inefficiencies in financial markets—would allow them to realize better expected growth opportunities, thereby resulting in large productivity gains.

The original findings in this volume have important implications for a range of financial sector policy interventions aimed at addressing the financing gaps for firms in EMDEs. The findings also provide strong analytical underpinnings for existing, *practical* knowledge in supporting SME financing. Furthermore, the exploration of novel databases sheds new light on long-standing challenges that are relevant for policy makers: how inefficiencies in financial markets constrain private firms in EMDEs, how these inefficiencies vary across firms of different sizes and ages, and the impact of financial constraints on growth and productivity. The volume also reveals, for the first time, the relevance of the composition of financing sources—namely, debt versus equity—for the productivity and growth of firms in EMDEs.

Nonetheless, there is still a lot to be learned about the relative merits of various sources of financing for firms and their potential complementarities, the relevance and effectiveness of specific policy interventions to address critical financing gaps, and the impact of the misallocation of finance on the productivity and growth of firms.[9] The volume thus concludes with a call for more research on these issues.

# Notes

1. See Carvajal and Didier (2024).

2. Zombie firms are firms that can stay afloat despite being unable to pay off their debt obligations and being unable to remain profitable in the long term. These firms typically have low productivity and are heavily indebted.

3. The limited depth of private markets for equity financing in EMDEs in the near term indicates that debt financing continues to be the key financing source for innovative firms, including those with investments in intangibles. However, the evidence in chapter 3 points to market failures and financial frictions in the use of intangible assets as collateral. Research in this area indicates that there are difficulties in valuing intangible assets and realizing any attributed value due to their limited liquidity and costly redeployment. The lack of pledgeability by outside investors further undermines the viability of intangible assets for debt contracts. There is limited empirical evidence on the effectiveness of specific policies supporting intangible assets collateralization for debt financing, especially in the context of EMDEs, which calls for more research on this topic. More research is needed on how policies could foster the use of intangible assets as collateral in debt financing. See, for example, Amable, Chatelain, and Ralf (2010); Brasell and Boschmans (2018); Brassell and King (2013); Crouzet et al. (2022); and Demmou and Franco (2021).

4. See, for example, World Bank (2019) for a more detailed discission on developing information systems in EMDEs.

5. See, for example, Calomiris et al. (2017); Campello and Larrain (2016); and Love, Martinez Peria, and Singh (2013).

6. The recently updated *Principles for Effective Insolvency and Creditor/Debtor Regimes* provides specific recommendations for the design of bankruptcy regimes for micro and small enterprises, including minimizing documentation requirements, keeping the debtor in control during restructuring, and simplifying the mechanisms of plan approval (World Bank 2021).

7. Research in this area indicates that there are difficulties in valuing intangible assets and realizing their attributed value due to their limited liquidity and costly redeployment, which render them a riskier and less valuable form of collateral.

8. Mirroring the approach in this volume, firm-level data are not only key for micro analytics, but also can complement and improve the understanding of macroeconomic diagnostics. Research has shown that changes in macroeconomic variables, at both the cyclical and secular frequencies, are best understood by tracking the evolution of economic variables at the firm level (Lagakos and Shu 2021; US National Research Council 2007).

9. Drawing insights from the experience of both HICs and EMDEs, Carvajal and Didier (2024) discuss how governments can enhance the effectiveness of their policies supporting SME access to finance.

# References

Amable, B., J. B. Chatelain, and K. Ralf. 2010. "Patents as Collateral." *Journal of Economic Dynamics and Control* 34 (6): 1092–104.

Bartlett, R., A. Morse, R. Stanton, and N. Wallace. 2022. "Consumer-Lending Discrimination in the FinTech Era." *Journal of Financial Economics* 143 (1): 30–56.

Brassell, M., and K. Boschmans. 2018. "Fostering the Use of Intangibles to Strengthen SME Access to Finance." OECD SME and Entrepreneurship Paper 12, Organisation for Economic Co-operation and Development, Paris.

Brassell, M., and K. King. 2013. "Banking on IP? The Role of Intellectual Property and Intangible Assets in Facilitating Business Finance." Intellectual Property Office of the United Kingdom, Newport South Wales, UK.

Calomiris, C. W., M. Larrain, J. Liberti, and J. Sturgess. 2017. "How Collateral Laws Shape Lending and Sectoral Activity." *Journal of Financial Economics* 123 (1): 163–88.

Campello, M., and M. Larrain. 2016. "Enlarging the Contracting Space: Collateral Menus, Access to Credit, and Economic Activity." *Review of Financial Studies* 29 (2): 349–83.

Carvajal, A. F., and T. Didier. 2024. "Boosting SME Finance and Growth: The Case for More Effective Support Policies." World Bank, Washington, DC.

CCAF (Cambridge Centre for Alternative Finance), World Bank, and World Economic Forum. 2022. "The Global Covid-19 Fintech Market Impact and Industry Resilience Report." University of Cambridge, World Bank Group, and World Economic Forum.

Crouzet, N., J. Eberly, A. Eisfoldt, and D. Papanikolaou. 2022. "The Economics of Intangible Capital." *Journal of Economic Perspectives* 36 (3): 29052.

Cumming, D. J., and S. A. Johan. 2019. *Crowdfunding: Fundamental Cases, Facts, and Insights.* Cambridge, MA: Academic Press.

Demmou, L., and G. Franco. 2021. "Mind the Financing Gap: Enhancing the Contribution of Intangible Assets to Productivity." OECD Economics Department Working Paper 1681, Organisation for Economic Co-operation and Development, Paris.

Didier, T., E. Feyen, R. Llovett-Montanes, and O. Ardic. 2022. "Global Patterns of Fintech Activity and Enabling Factors: Fintech and the Future of Finance Flagship Technical Note." World Bank, Washington, DC.

Farag, H., and S. Johan. 2021. "How Alternative Finance Informs Central Themes in Corporate Finance." *Journal of Corporate Finance* 67: 101879.

Guenther, C., S. Johan, and D. Schweizer. 2018. "Is the Crowd Sensitive to Distance? How Investment Decisions Differ by Investor Type." *Small Business Economics* 50 (2): 289–305.

Lagakos, D., and M. Shu. 2021. "The Role of Micro Data in Understanding Structural Transformation." STEG Pathfinding Paper, Structural Transformation and Economic Growth, Oxford, UK.

Lerner, J., and R. Nanda. 2020. "Venture Capital's Role in Financing Innovation: What We Know and How Much We Still Need to Learn." *Journal of Economic Perspectives* 34 (3): 23–61.

Love, I., M. S. Martinez Peria, and S. Singh. 2013. "Collateral Registries for Movable Assets: Does Their Introduction Spur Firms' Access to Bank Finance?" Policy Research Working Paper 6477, World Bank, Washington, DC.

Strausz, R. 2017. "A Theory of Crowdfunding: A Mechanism Design Approach with Demand Uncertainty and Moral Hazard." *American Economic Review* 107 (6): 1430–76.

US National Research Council. 2007. *Understanding Business Dynamics: An Integrated Data System for America's Future.* Washington, DC: National Academies Press.

World Bank. 2019. "Credit Reporting Knowledge Guide 2019." World Bank, Washington, DC.

World Bank. 2021. *Principles for Effective Insolvency and Creditor/Debtor Regimes.* Washington, DC: World Bank.